ERIKA

ERIKA
What Can Man Do To Me?

as told to

LOTHAR VON SELTMANN

Translated from the German by
Damaris Walter and Richard Herkes

David C Cook

First published in German 2005
Copyright © R. Brockhaus Verlag Wuppertal 2005

English translation first published 2009
Copyright © Kingsway Communications 2009

Published by David C. Cook
Kingsway Communications Ltd
26–28 Lottbridge Drove, Eastbourne BN23 6NT, UK

David C. Cook
4050 Lee Vance View, Colorado Springs, CO 80918, USA

David C. Cook Distribution Canada
55 Woodslee Avenue, Paris, Ontario, Canada N3L 3E5

David C. Cook and the graphic circle C logo
are registered trademarks of Cook Communications Ministries.

Biblical quotations are from The Holy Bible: New International Version
© 1973, 1978, 1984 by the International Bible Society.

ISBN 978 1 84291 318 5

Cover design by PinnacleCreative.co.uk

Typeset in India by Alliance Data Technology

Printed in Italy
1 2 3 4 5 13 12 11 10 09

Contents

1.	Bombed Out	7
2.	The Road to Danzig	25
3.	The Russians Are Coming!	51
4.	Deported	67
5.	Life at Camp	87
6.	Moving On	105
7.	Coming Home	125
8.	Working on the Farm	141
9.	A Surprising Encounter	159
10.	Gifts from God	175
	Afterword	185

CHAPTER I

Bombed Out

It was May 1944, a beautiful spring day in Hörde just outside of Dortmund. The sun shone from a cloudless sky, seemingly undisturbed by the smoke and dirt that drifted from the nearby factories of the Hösch Corporation. It bathed houses and streets, yards and gardens, in a friendly hue. Vapours drifted towards the city centre, across the workers' residential district in the south-eastern part of town. The day was bright and warm, filled with the song of blackbird and thrush, finch and starling, all darting about the green bushes or up into some convenient tree. The air was replete with the humming and buzzing of bees and other insects, all feasting on the blossoms of apple, pear and plum trees in the tiny back gardens. And, here and there, the happy voices of children flitted across the streets and around the houses.

This was a quiet part of town – no squeaking trams, no roaring buses, hardly even a motor car to disturb the tranquillity. Occasionally you might hear the shrill steam whistle of a passing freight train, but not so as anyone would notice.

You could be forgiven for thinking this was a place of peace. But the German Reich was at war. In fact, the whole world was at

war, even if you couldn't see that here in Hörde, far from the
bombs and gunfire. Death was never far away; in more than one
home this lovely spring day offered its cheer in vain.

Apart from the children playing in the streets, there were few
people to be seen. The men that were fit for military service had
gone off in all directions, away at one of the fronts or on some
military base. And if they weren't away on some sortie risking
their lives for their homeland, they were at work – most of them
in the factories of the Hösch Corporation.

The women were needed too, playing their part during the
day, even though that meant leaving the children – unless they
were very young and there was no Grandma to step in. This was
how it was for the Remplins in Beukenberg Street. Here Greta,
who was Mum, took care of the modest house and small garden.
It was one of the few detached homes in the area. They'd bought
it five years ago. It had a solid foundation with an arched cellar,
underneath one-and-a-half storeys of scoria brick, with enough
rooms for the six members of the family. Greta had been given
leave from work so she could take care of the children. Siegfried,
the youngest, was four years old; Hildegard was almost six; and
Hellmuth was eight. But Erika was already seventeen. She was an
elegant young woman, a pupil at the renowned Eicker Dancing
School in Dortmund, and naturally an able help to her mother
when she got back from school each day.

Dad was Arthur, a policeman. He had already been on a
special mission in Austria for several months. Nobody in the
family knew exactly what kind of mission it was – Arthur was a
quiet man at the best of times, and he'd hardly said a word about
it. Sadly now he was almost never at home: the family were left
to go it alone. And, with the enemy gaining the upper hand,

the war was beginning to stretch its murderous claws even as far as peaceful Hörde.

Greta stopped working in the garden and sat for a moment on the small bench under the flowering lilac. She enjoyed the sun's warmth, the scent and the sounds of spring. Her two younger children were playing quietly in the sandpit. Her eldest son was evidently out in the streets playing football with the other boys: even from here, behind the house, she could hear them plainly. And then she heard Erika, humming a tune as she came dancing into the garden with her light and rhythmical steps. She did a pirouette in front of her mother, coming to a halt with a perfect *effacé*. In her right hand she was carrying a light sweater.

'Well done! I know you'll pass your exam.'

'I think so, too, Mamá,' Erika replied, sounding the second syllable as if she were French. 'And then I'll be a ballerina. But now I have to go.'

'Where are you going? I didn't know you were—'

'The girls from the BDM[1] are waiting for me,' Erika cut in. She gave her *Mamá* a kiss and turned to go, and now her mother noticed that she was wearing the dark skirt, white blouse and scarf of her uniform. 'Please, be back by seven o'clock. I have a meeting tonight. And put on your sweater if it gets any colder.'

'I will, *Mamá*. I'll be back on time. Adieu!' Erika called over her shoulder and disappeared behind the house.

Hildegard came over from the sandpit. 'I wish I could dance like her, Mummy!' She adored her older sister.

---

[1] The *Bund Deutscher Mädchen*, Federation of German Girls.

'Yes, Erika is very talented,' Greta told her young daughter. 'Maybe she'll be a real ballerina some day. As for you, we'll see how you get on when you're older. But first you have to grow up! And our Führer Adolf Hitler and his brave soldiers have to win the war.'

Just then Siegfried joined them. 'When will the Führer win the war? And when will Erika become a ballerina?'

'Hopefully soon, my little one,' his mother replied. 'And then your daddy will come back home and be a policeman here in Dortmund.'

'Yes, I want Daddy to come home,' the boy stomped on the ground. 'I can hardly remember what he looks like!'

Greta sighed. 'I'm sure he'll be home soon.' Her sigh belied her words – as the children missed their father, so she missed her husband. If only he'd contact them more often . . . if only this war could be won soon! Greta was a loyal follower of the Führer, but her doubts were growing over whether his grand ideas would ever be reality. The sacrifices were ever greater. So far she and her family had been spared. So far.

Erika came back on time from her meeting, as excited as ever. She found them all sitting eating at the kitchen table. Her cheerful 'Salut! Bonsoir!' rang awkwardly in the muted atmosphere.

'You know I don't like your French greetings, Erika,' her mother chided. 'We still say Heil Hitler. Remember that!'

'I'm sorry, Mamá,' Erika pouted, adding a rather mumbled Heil Hitler on the end. 'But you all look like the cat stole your milk! What's up?' It was only then she noticed the bags and suitcases on the floor. 'Oh. Are we taking a trip somewhere?'

'We have to sleep in the cellar tonight,' Siegfried announced. Erika didn't understand and turned to her mother for clarification:

'Actually, we're not going to sleep in the cellar tonight, but we ought to pack our bags and suitcases just in case. There were warnings of air raids for the Ruhr area on the radio again.' She sighed. 'The enemy gives us no rest. So if the sirens go we have to go down. I've already got some things ready – we must be prepared for the worst. I've chosen things for the two younger ones. You can pack them while I'm out at my meeting. And please pack your own and Hellmuth's bag as well. Oh, and clean up the kitchen before that.'

'All right, I will, Mamá,' replied Erika, as she sat to the table for a slice of bread and a cup of tea. Her mother got up, a little shakily Erika thought, and sighed again. 'And don't keep addressing me in French! The French are not on our side. I don't like it. A German girl ought to say "Máma" or "Mother".'

'Okay, okay, Mother,' Erika replied stroppily. 'But French is the language of dance! And I'm going to be a dancer, *Mother*.'

Greta didn't react to her daughter's remark, or the way she emphasised the last word. She put her jacket on and said goodbye to her children, giving each one a quick kiss. 'Don't go to bed too late – and sleep well.'

'And we really don't have to go down to the cellar?' Hellmuth was looking for reassurance.

'The air-raid siren gives us enough time,' his mother replied on her way out.

Erika stayed with the children till she had finished eating, and then she cleaned up the kitchen and packed Siegfried's and Hildegard's suitcases. Then she gathered them all back round the table to tell them an exciting bedtime story and to sing them their favourite lullaby:

Heidschi Bumbeidschi, sleep deep and long,
Your mother has gone and will not return.

She leaves the wee lad all on his own.
Heidschi Bumbeidschi, boom-diddy-boom,
Heidschi Bumbeidschi, boom-diddy-boom.

After she'd put the two little ones to bed she helped Hellmuth pack his bags and then he went off to bed. Now the young ballerina could gather up all the bits and pieces she felt she needed . . . obviously her ballet shoes – too bad the tutu was too bulky to fit in the bag. But never fear – the radio announcer hadn't said anything that night on the nine o'clock news that would make any difference to the Ruhr. So no need to worry.

And, as it turned out, everything did remain calm that night, and the cellar stayed empty.

But not the next night. For the first time in the district sirens were heard. They went off around ten, and repeated their eerie howl soon after. So this time the family really did have to sleep in the makeshift shelter that was their cellar.

Evidently things were getting serious for Dortmund and its outlying districts. And Hörde was sure to be in trouble, surrounded as it was by several industrial complexes like the Hösch Corporation. No doubt these were the targets of the enemy planes, rather than the residential areas. But then again . . . in the darkness of the night, were the bombers really going to be able to distinguish coal-mines, barracks and factories? And what if their aim *was* the civil population? Erika did not feel like sleeping.

'When will this war really be over?' she asked her mother when the two of them were quietly talking. The younger children were already fast asleep on their makeshift beds. For them, this night was a bit of an adventure.

'As soon as the Führer has won the war.' Greta's response was meant to sound convincing. It did not. Erika summoned her courage and gave voice to her doubts: 'Do you really believe in the ultimate victory, Mother?'

'We have to. Hitler has promised it to us. And he keeps his promises.' Greta tried to sound confident. 'We have no right to doubt this,' she added. Fortunately for her the two women couldn't see each other in the darkness, or Erika would have seen that the confidence her mother had put into her words was not to be found in her eyes.

'I'm not so sure about it any more, Mamá,' Erika pressed. 'There are too many people dying, and too much has been destroyed by these bombs. Just look at Düsseldorf and Hamm, and of course Berlin over and over again. And I bet there's a lot more we don't even know about. And what about the front lines? How many women have become widows? And how many children have lost their fathers?' The agitation in her voice was even more obvious in the darkness.

'Those sacrifices are necessary, Erika,' was the only answer that came. 'They are inevitable. No war has ever been won without sacrifice. You must not have doubts about the Führer's victory!'

'And what if we are affected? What if Papá doesn't return from Austria? Or what if a bomb falls on our house and buries us down here?'

Greta hesitated. Finally she affirmed, 'Then we have to accept it . . . as our sacrifice for the Führer and his victory.' But she couldn't help the tremor in her voice. Was that anger at the impertinence of Erika's questions, or was she beginning to worry that her daughter could be right? Either way, she didn't react to the outraged response that came. She merely listened, without acknowledging the anger and the fear.

'How can you talk and think like that, Mamá? It hurts. I don't want to die for Hitler and his ideas! I'm only seventeen – I want to live, and I want to become a dancer!'

She sobbed into her pillow, and still her mother did not react. She had her own struggle going on, as conviction clashed with doubt.

Everything remained calm that night. They heard the sirens just once more, and that was to signal the all-clear. For Hellmuth, Hildegard and Siegfried the taste of adventure was intact. Sleeping in the cellar with only one oil lamp, just boards and blankets to sleep on, was exciting. It reminded them of the times when their dad had taken them camping. But Greta and Erika could sense the unseen damage that their argument had done to their relationship.

The next day passed much as the previous one, except for the tense atmosphere that had developed. The next night had to be spent down in the cellar again, after the radio's warning to everyone in the eastern Ruhr. At ten o'clock the sirens sounded more insistently, or so it seemed to Erika. Soon the night was filled with the thundering of countless aeroplane engines. Then came the explosions, followed time after time by the rhythmical thundering of anti-aircraft fire. Sometimes it was fairly faint, dulled by distance; at other times it came near, growing louder, frightening in its ferocity.

The Remplin family sat huddled together in the cellar with their oil lamp and held each other's hands. There was no way they could sleep. With each new thunder blast they cowered, as if to shield themselves against things that might come down on them at any moment. The hours passed, and still they'd not been hit. Greta tried hard to calm the two youngest, who had started whimpering after the first near-misses. Erika took care of Hellmuth, who tried to be brave despite his fear. She talked to him quietly, trying to distract him with stories from the dancing school and her missions with the BDM. And all the while she tried to conceal her own fear.

For a while things seemed to calm down outside, but then new planes could be heard moving in again. Engines roared even louder – and then, suddenly, a clap of thunder shook the house, so loud they thought their eardrums would burst. A shockwave flung the door open against the wall. Somehow it stayed in one piece.

A thick cloud of dust was blown into the room. They coughed as they fought for breath. Amazingly the lamp stayed alight. Then they heard ominous rumblings above them, and felt heavy items falling, as though the whole place were falling in on them. Plaster rained down. Then, silence.

They managed to close the door, and after a while the dust settled. Soon they could see the arched cellar ceiling, which had amazingly held out against the battering from above.

Eventually they could make out the distant roar of aeroplane engines as they faded into a gloomy silence. No one made a sound. No one moved. Questions were nursed in silence.

As Greta held Siegfried and Hildegard in her arms, both trembling with fear, an old lament came into her mind. And so she started to sing, declaring her own war on the silence and the fear.

In a silent hour at the night's first watch
a voice took up a lament:

The night's cool wind had carried the sound
　　with soft and swift intent.
Its song was sad, it broke my heart
　　all through the midnight hours;
My tears ran down, my tears ran free
　　and watered all the flowers.
The lovely moon is dipping low,
　　for sorrow's sake she flees,
While sparkling stars now cease to shine:
　　they want to weep with me.
No birdsong now, nor merry sound
　　is coming on the breeze,
But all creation mourns with me
　　amid the mountain trees.[2]

Greta didn't know why this song had come into her mind . . .
perhaps it was a premonition of the sorrow waiting for them
upstairs. Had this night changed all their lives? She didn't know,
but for the moment she was just glad her song had calmed her
children. They all sat quietly, waiting for events to unfold.

Still holding Hellmuth in her arms, Erika was the first to break
the silence. 'What shall we do now, Mother?'

'Let's just wait a little longer, and then I'll go upstairs and have
a look. You never know, there might be more planes coming.
There hasn't been an all-clear yet. We're safer down here.'

'I wonder what time it is,' Erika said.

'It must be nearly dawn. Maybe we should try to get some sleep.'

As Siegfried and Hildegard slept soundly, worn out by the
recent terrors, the other three tried to get some rest.

---

[2] Friedrich von Spee, from the folk collection *Zupfgeigenhansl.*

Greta was the first to wake. She could hear somebody outside calling her name, over and over again: 'Greta, Greta, where are you? Please, if you're still in there, come out quickly!'

Carefully, so as not to wake the two children in her arms, she stood to her feet. It was time to see what had happened in the night. Clearly many of her neighbours had come out with the same idea, and they were starting to worry about Greta.

'Be careful, Mother.' Erika had just woken up. 'Should I come with you?'

'Stay down here with the others. Someone should be there when they wake up. I'll be right back.'

She lay the children down, and then, as quietly as possible, opened the door. She gazed up the stairway through a dense fog into a bright morning. She must have been asleep for quite a while. The air smelled of burning.

The sting of smoke made her eyes water. Where was that coming from? Hurriedly she now climbed the stairs, which were all covered with debris.

Their little garden, the lilac bush, the vegetable patch, the sandpit . . . everything was covered in a thin layer of dust. But wait – a piece of the house was missing! It had been torn off and spread all over the ground. Yet unbelievably the cellar had remained undamaged! The shock of how close death had come to them suddenly hit her, and she cried out. And that wasn't her last cry, as she turned round and saw the house in ruins, some parts still on fire.

From downstairs Erika called out, 'What is it, Mamá?' Now she too climbed the stairs, and screamed as she came out into the day. Not that she had seen their own house yet – it was the remains of the neighbour's that caught her eye. There was nothing but a smoking heap of rubble. People were scrabbling about, looking for their neighbours. Then Erika turned to see her own house, and gasped.

By now Anna, a neighbour from over the road, had noticed them. She was the one who had been calling Greta's name, only she had obviously given up when nobody had answered. She clambered over the rubble. 'Greta, Erika, you're alive! Thank God, you're alive! We thought you . . . hadn't made it. Where are the children?'

The two women hugged each other. 'All of us survived, Anna. And none of us are hurt. The little ones are still asleep in the cellar.' Her voice trembled.

'I have to tell the others that you're alive!' Anna exclaimed as she turned to go, adding: 'There's nothing you can do to save your house, I'm afraid.' Then she was gone.

Greta and Erika tried to get the measure of what was left of their house. It was nothing but a heap of rubble, the crackling flames still eating away the last remains. They had simply had no idea down in the cellar just how bad the damage was. But the fire had not reached them! Half the roof was gone, one whole end of the house had collapsed – right next to the neighbouring house which had been completely destroyed – and all the other walls were damaged as well. Not a single window or door had remained intact; a large chunk of the end wall lay in the drive-way. Pieces of charred furniture were scattered everywhere. All they could see was one horrible, burning, smoking chaos.

It was the morning of the 25th May 1944. Without a word the two women hugged each other and allowed their tears to flow.

Greta broke the silence. 'Our beautiful house, gone, just bombed out and burned down! Aagh, those wretched Yanks!

Those Tommies! They're pigs, the lot of them! What's to become of us now? If Arthur knew about this . . .'

'But, Mamá, we're alive! None of us were hurt. All five of us are safe and sound. Just imagine what would have happened if the fire had got down into the cellar . . . or if it had blocked our way out! It's only the house that's gone . . . only things.' She pressed on through her mother's sobs. 'Look at the poor Koslowskis over the road. They've had a direct hit by the looks of it. I wonder if any of them have survived at all.'

'No one survived over there. They were all killed.' Greta and Erika jumped – they hadn't noticed that Anna had come back.

'Weren't they in the cellar?' Erika exclaimed.

'Yes, they were,' Anna choked a reply. 'But the bomb went right through the house to the ground below. Direct hit . . . and all the fire brigades in Dortmund are busy. It must be even worse there. There was no one here who could put the fire out. Damned war!'

The woman wiped the tears from her face. Erika felt her own tears returning, but when Anna asked again about the children, she quickly recovered. 'They must still be asleep – they don't have a clue what's going on up here. I'll go back down.'

Erika disappeared over the heaps of rubble, and moments later returned with three drowsy children all rubbing their eyes. At last the whole family stood in the garden, gazing in silence at the smoking ruin. They let the tears flow.

'Our beautiful house,' Hildegard moaned. 'Our home . . . it's completely destroyed!'

'Where are we supposed to live now?' Hellmuth asked, as he stared with big, wet eyes at the ruins and the flames.

Siegfried stomped on the ground, as he always did when he wasn't happy about something. 'Change it back! Those horrible people, dropping bombs . . . This all has to be put back again! I want Daddy! He'll have to punish them, and make the fire go away, and put the house back together again.'

Greta ruffled his curly hair. 'You're right, my little one, Daddy will have to come home soon. And then we'll put the house back together again, all of us together.' She kept her doubts buried.

Just then Hellmuth piped up. 'There's fire everywhere – how come the fire brigade's not here?'

'Anna said that they've got to put the fires out in Dortmund. I suppose our fire is too small,' Erika replied weakly.

'But they have to put the fire out! We've got to live somewhere!' protested her little brother.

'The flames will go out soon. And we'll find somewhere to stay,' Erika reassured him. 'We won't have to stay and sleep outside.'

'Yes, come along. Somebody's sure to help us,' Greta put in, now sounding more convincing. 'We'll sort this out later. Right now we should be happy . . . and thankful that we're better off than the Koslowskis. They all died. We're alive – without so much as a scratch! And, remember, we've still got some things left, down in the cellar.'

'It was because of our arched cellar and the strong scoria bricks that we were saved,' Hellmuth declared. 'Vaults are far more solid than flat wooden ceilings. And scoria bricks are fireproof.'

'Or maybe it was providence,' Greta added. She was thinking how the Führer had constantly felt preserved from conspiracies and attacks by providence. 'Yes, providence,' she said again. 'And I'm sure that it will save us in the future, too.'

'I'd rather be guarded by God than by some kind of providence,' Erika mumbled, talking more to herself than her mother, who said nothing. And at that moment Erika recalled her confirmation

Bible verse from three years before, when she was fourteen. It was from Psalm 118:6–7.

> The Lord is with me; I will not be afraid.
> What can man do to me?
> The Lord is with me; he is my helper.

But Erika dismissed the thought as quickly as it came. Like her parents, she had cared little for church or faith before her confirmation, and even less afterwards. She wasn't even interested in the teachings of the so-called 'German Christians' who were loyal to the Führer. For Erika's family there simply was no God. So how could he have anything to do with what happened to them last night?

They stayed in the garden for quite a while, their eyes now resigned to the chaos around them. The fine spring day went by unnoticed. Despite the warmth they shivered, only too glad that they had taken their jackets with them when they'd first gone into the cellar. Standing outside now, they scarcely noticed the damage to the rest of the street, or the group of people that had gathered some way away from the ruins. Their eyes were fixed on the remains of their own house. The flames were beginning to die down now, as they ran out of stuff to burn and succumbed to the buckets of water being thrown over them. A human chain of neighbours had formed – although, try as they might, they didn't manage to save anything.

Greta, Erika and Hellmuth wanted to look through the ruins themselves, in the vain hope that some of their things had survived. But it was too dangerous – a ceiling might collapse at any moment. Now there would be no toys for the little ones; and no tutu for

Erika, for the ballet dance she was due to perform soon. Even the crockery and cutlery was ruined. The only things left to them now were what they had taken down to the cellar.

Happily Greta had taken what jewellery she had with her, as well as their most important documents. And, she reflected, was I not the person talking only days ago about the sacrifices we may have to make for the Führer and his final victory? How much worse it all could have been! But thanks to providence, the sacrifice was bearable . . .

As time went on people kept coming over to celebrate their escape – unlike the poor Koslowskis. Someone brought food and drink, and they soon found that people's thoughtfulness lifted their spirits. Then at last somebody from the local Red Cross appeared, expressing his regret over the family's terrible circumstances and ready to sort out where they could stay for a while. Were there perhaps family or friends in other parts of the town or in nearby cities who would be willing to accommodate them? In response Greta suggested an aunt who lived in the southern part of Bochum. She ought to have room in her flat. And from there Greta could organise the rebuilding. The man agreed on the plan and said that the family would be given a lift to Bochum in the afternoon. It would be no problem, especially with so little baggage . . .

Greta agreed to be at the station in Hörde at three o'clock with her children and the few belongings left to them, hoping that the aunt would be willing to take them in. Then all that remained was to keep out of the ruins and resign herself to their loss. As it was, she soon learned that the centre of Dortmund had been hit far more severely than Hörde. This was clearly the time for sacrifices . . .

At three in the afternoon Greta was at the station with her children and their few bits and pieces. From there they were taken to their surprised aunt, who nevertheless agreed to house the homeless. It was clearly going to be quite cramped for all of them. Yet the aunt said that it would be all right, since she was only doing her duty as a Christian.

CHAPTER 2

The Road to Danzig

Aunt Erna's apartment was tiny. The six of them (seven at night, when Aunt Erna's daughter Wiltraud was home from the office) had to make the best of it. There was nowhere outside where the children could play, as Aunt Erna had no garden and there was too much traffic on the street in front of the house. The children spent most of their time indoors.

Hellmuth was annoyed that he had to go to a different school. He didn't know any of the children there and thought everyone was stupid, including the teachers.

As for Erika, the route to her dancing school was now a long and complex one. She had to leave the house very early in the morning and come back late in the afternoon. Public transport to Dortmund had never been that good, but with the bombing it was far worse than usual. She had to change twice: from tram to train and again to another tram. And to top it all, she now had no barre at which to practise her various positions and steps.

Nor could she see her friends from the BDM any more, and there were no new friends around here. She felt like crying. Why did this war have to ruin everything? She pinned her hopes on at least being able to take her dancing exam, though her teacher had indicated that she didn't know how much longer she'd be able to keep the school open in these turbulent times. Was this the end of all Erika's dreams of being a ballerina?

Something else soon caused dissension in their new, cramped lodgings. Aunt Erna was a devout woman who belonged to the professing church, which was against union with National Socialism. She always had a Bible and hymn book lying on her table; not for her a portrait of the Führer, or any other member of the Nazi élite, nor any of the political sayings which had decorated the walls back in Hörde. And there certainly wasn't any room on her shelves for Hitler's *Mein Kampf.*

Aunt Erna insisted on praying before and after each meal, as she'd always done. Before breakfast she would read a text from her *Book of Watchwords*, with texts from the Bible for each day. After dinner she would read from the Bible, following a reading plan from the Prussian Bible Society printed at the back. And sometimes she would also read a thought for the day from a calendar. It wasn't easy for her Nazi guests to grasp that the texts talked about the Jews and about Jesus Christ, who was supposed to be Lord of all things, and who claimed to be God's Son, and who was supposed to have deliberately let himself be crucified.

It was so completely un-German, what their aunt was doing – and what she was expecting them to do. The 'Israelites' were Jews, and everyone knew what to make of them: the whole of the Old Testament with its ethics of reward and punishment ought to be burned! And the New Testament was just full of distorted and superstitious reports on the Jew called Jesus. If he'd at least been heroic, that would be something . . . but no, this was the religion of a loser for losers. No way did this fit with Nazi principles and ideas. It may have been all well and good for weak, non-Aryan souls, but a true German didn't waste time on it.

So Erika had learned from her BDM leaders. And Greta, who was a leader herself, had persistently reminded her children of this – even with Erika's confirmation three years earlier, which had been nothing more than a necessary formality in the German Christian community.

Aunt Erna, however, would not change her mind when Greta and Erika confronted her. Tall and imposing, she faced them squarely: 'You'll see who'll win out in the end,' she said firmly. 'Do not be deceived: God will not be mocked. A man reaps what he sows,' she insisted, quoting the book of Galatians. 'And you seem to have reaped from what your Führer has sown already . . . You ought to wake up before it's too late.'

Greta refused to let Aunt Erna's beliefs get to her. She held on tightly to her Nazi convictions and defended them, especially when it came to matters of religion. Though she didn't dare press the point too much, as she knew she needed Erna's help, she couldn't help herself on one occasion: 'Maybe it would have been better if we'd stayed in our cellar instead of troubling you with our German ways!' Aunt Erna listened, and responded only with a sympathetic look, as if to say, 'Poor thing, by the time you understand it will be too late.'

But before very long Erika began to open up to her great-aunt and became more tentative in her approach. She was, after all, old enough to have a mind of her own, not least when it came to war and peace.

It was hard for everyone to get along, but it wasn't in fact to last long. After just ten days Greta returned from a visit to the city council with amazing news: 'By the beginning of next week I'll be taking the children to Gosslershausen in the Danzig district. My mother needs me; plus, they still have peace over there in West Prussia. The countryside is away from the war, and I'll be able to do something useful for the Führer and the fatherland – and show the polacks what work is!'

'Oh yes, let's go and see Grandma!' Hellmuth cried excitedly. 'I can't even remember what she looks like. I wonder if she still has those fat pigs.' His younger brother and sister chimed in. 'We're going to Grandma Luise; we're going to Grandma Luise!' they chanted as they danced around the living room.

But Erika was not so sure. 'To Grandma Luise? I'm not coming, Mother. I'll stay with Aunt Erna so I can keep going to dancing school. I must take my exam!'

Greta bit her lip and simply told the other two to calm down. She thought for a moment. Was it a good idea to leave her daughter with this woman? What influence might she have on the immature Erika? But finally she agreed: 'All right, if Aunt Erna agrees to let you stay here, you may finish your school first. But then you must come too. There'll be opportunities enough for dancing later.' She cast a questioning glance towards her aunt.

'I'd love to have Erika stay here with me,' said Erna. 'There'll definitely be enough room here for the three of us, even for quite a long period. You go ahead to West Prussia. Luise will be happy to have you there. Who knows what will happen after that? Only God knows.' Aunt Erna's faith in providence, if that was what it was, got a disapproving look from her niece, but she made no response. For the time being at least, their destinies were set.

Two days later it was time to say farewell. Greta took Hellmuth, Hildegard and Siegfried and started out on what was sure to be a long and arduous journey. They would travel via Hannover, Berlin and Posen, leaving Erika in Bochum. Greta's heart was heavy. The news on the radio and in the newspapers gave no hint of the victory they hoped was just around the corner. On the contrary, the news from the east was bad – and that was precisely where she was headed. Not that things were any better in the west. An invasion of American and British troops was apparently imminent, though nobody knew where the enemy would strike first.

At the station Greta hugged her daughter for one last time, forcing confidence into her voice: 'Take care, my child. And don't listen to any of Aunt Erna's religious nonsense. The victory is ours! *Heil Hitler!*' She joined her children on board the train and waved her handkerchief through the open window. She continued to wave until the train had left the station, puffing and pounding, when it finally disappeared in its own cloud of smoke.

Erika and Aunt Erna stood on the platform and waved. Erika held a handkerchief to her face, unable to fight back the tears. This was the first time she had been parted from her family for more than a week. Now she had no idea when she'd see them again. Aunt Erna gave her a hug. 'Don't be sad,' she consoled. 'They'll have a safe journey. God will be with them. And the two of us will get along just fine.'

'But Mamá doesn't believe in God, Aunt Erna; she believes in the Führer and in providence!' Erika croaked through her tears. 'I mean, you don't believe in the Führer or providence, do you?' Only now, alone with her aunt, did she dare ask the question.

Erna took Erika's hand and looked into her eyes. 'I don't put my trust in any vague kind of providence, and I don't put my trust in people, Erika. I trust in the true God, in the Saviour

Jesus Christ. The Führer – as Adolf Hitler wants to be called – is a man who has pronounced himself God – and there are many who worship him as a god. This isn't right, and it will be his undoing in the end. I'm convinced that within a year from now this "thousand-year kingdom" he goes on about will have been completely destroyed. "Blessed is he whose Führer is God," the song goes, and that's what I believe.'

'Have you any idea what you're saying?' Erika asked, as they left the station. She was clearly shocked, and then she added stubbornly, 'The Führer Adolf Hitler will find a way. Victory is ours! Just like Mamá said!'

'Calm down, dear. I understand. This is the BDM talking, not to mention your family. I just don't want you to be disappointed if things don't turn out that way. Remember what I said before: "Don't be deceived: God will not be mocked." I hope the German people come to realise this before we have a disaster on our hands.'

'Are you trying to scare me, Aunt?' Erika asked.

'I don't want to scare you, child. But I do want to warn you. Things don't look good for the German Reich. Their propaganda is just spreading lies and misleading the people. Something terrible is about to happen, I'm sure of it – somewhere around the English Channel, or in France or Belgium. The Americans, the British and the Canadians will all be here before long. The German troops in France and Belgium won't stand a chance against them. Trust me. May God have mercy on all of us. Now, let's get home and start our new life.'

The two women did get on well enough: they could have been grandmother and granddaughter. There were no problems with Wiltraud either, whom Erika found to be less religious than her mother. Erika soon began to adapt to her aunt's way of life, and soon came to appreciate the way Erna coped with the hardships and constrictions of war. She was always so calm, seemingly unafraid of the nights of bombings, despite the death and destruction all around.

'I agree with the songwriter Paul Fleming,' she would often say, when the sirens sounded and people blacked out their windows and made for the bunkers and shelters. 'And what did he say?' Erika asked. At which her aunt would oblige with a song:

> Nothing will happen to me
> But what God has already seen
> And what is a blessing to me.
> I gladly accept his good will,
> And that which He asks of me still
> I choose to have and to be.
> I put my trust in His grace
> And gladly look to his face
> To shield me from all harm.
> If I live in line with his word
> Then nothing will damage or hurt
> But always I'll rest in his arms.

'I wish I had your faith,' said Erika, though she immediately regretted it. It was simply not appropriate for a girl of the BDM to wish anything of the sort, let alone say it out loud. She did not want to break the vow she had given the Führer. And anyway, he was sure to win. Hadn't he only recently (thanks to providence) survived an assault from a cowardly band of conspirators, a 'small group of ambitious, unscrupulous, criminal, stupid officers'? Hadn't this only confirmed his mission, proving that he really was the legitimate Führer of the German Reich and the German people; and the traitors would receive their just punishment.

It was the evening of July 20th. 'Oh, Erika,' Aunt Erna sighed. 'This was not a good day for Germany.'

Erika leapt from her chair. 'How can you say that, Aunt Erna! What would become of our Reich if Hitler had been assassinated? Tell me that!'

'Now, now, calm down, Erika. It's a fair question . . . what *would* become of the Reich and the war, the thousands of deaths at the front, the awful destruction in the cities, the countless victims across the country? Well, I for one believe that all that would soon come to an end. Think – no more sirens! People could begin to rebuild what's been destroyed by Hitler's policies and this dreadful war. Though it'll take a long time . . .'

Erika's voice faltered. 'Don't let anybody else know that you think this way, Aunt Erna. It could be dangerous for you.'

'I know, I know,' the old woman nodded. 'But I'm not afraid. I trust in the Lord. What can man do to me? That's what David says in Psalm 56. And I'll live by it, no matter what.'

Erika's eyes opened in amazement – not because her aunt's words seemed improper, the way they often did when they were discussing Hitler or the future of the German Reich. No, these were the very words from her confirmation just three years before, and the verse she was given at that time:

> The Lord is with me; I will not be afraid.
> What can man do to me?
> The Lord is with me; he is my helper.[1]

Erika remembered a card with a picture of the Rainoldi church in Dortmund, with this very Bible verse on it – it had probably been

---

[1] Psalm 118:6–7

burned in May along with everything else. Yet the words had been engraved in her memory, and now they suddenly revived.

Erika was troubled. She was a member of the BDM. She had pledged her loyalty to the Führer. And yet . . . she was becoming increasingly doubtful that Hitler's plans could be realised and final victory achieved. Aunt Erna might not be so mistaken.

Saying nothing, the seventeen-year-old left the lounge and went to her room. She needed to be alone with her thoughts, even if they were disturbing. How was she going to solve the huge dilemma before it tore her in two? Over the following weeks her sense of duty went to war with a growing inclination to agree with her aunt, and turn towards the Christian faith.

Meanwhile disasters great and small were occurring, inside the Reich and outside its borders, as it tried to enforce its will through the destruction of cities and the shedding of blood. And all this became the background to Erika's struggles, preparing her to look elsewhere for direction in life.

At the end of September, two things happened to change her course. First, her dancing teacher in Dortmund informed her pupils with a heavy heart that she would have to close the school, at least for the time being. The current situation left no room for the arts. Dancers now had different responsibilities. Some theatres had already been closed, including the famous Scala in Berlin, and the musicians were all employed in the defence industry. She tried to reassure them that there'd be work for ballet dancers again as soon as things improved, when their lessons could resume.

The other event was a letter from her mother, saying she ought to come as soon as possible. Greta needed her help at home there and in her grandma's small hotel. Grandma was in her seventies now and officially entitled to an assistant. Greta herself had taken on a job 'for the German Reich' and so couldn't manage without Erika's help any longer.

Erika shed some tears over leaving, but she knew what she had to do. And with her dream of becoming a ballerina now on hold, there was less reason to stay. She knew she would miss Aunt Erna – not least her faith in God during the bad times – but she began to look forward to seeing her family again. Not that anyone knew where her father was. None of them had received any news about him at all.

Erika packed her suitcase and bought a ticket, ready for the long trip to West Prussia. She planned to leave very early the next day.

'Put on your BDM uniform,' Aunt Erna advised. She nodded her affirmation when Erika gave her an astonished look. 'The blouse and the scarf may protect you. You're a pretty young woman. Who knows what kind of riff-raff will be hanging around on the train? Anyway, it's good, biblical counsel.'

Erika did not understand.

'"Use worldly wealth to gain friends for yourselves," it says somewhere in Luke.[2] You are a member of the BDM so you can show your loyalty to the Führer.'

'Actually I'm not sure I'm as loyal to the Führer as I used to be, Aunt Erna . . . The time I've had with you has got me thinking. Sometimes I'd just like to quit this whole Nazi business. It just doesn't seem . . .' Erika faltered.

Aunt Erna answered, 'You're right, of course. Eventually you will have to abandon the whole Nazi way of thinking, when it all falls to pieces. But still, right now I advise you to wear your uniform – at least the blouse and scarf under your coat.'

---

[2] Luke 16:9

Erika thanked her for the advice and went to get ready.

And so, early one grey September morning, the two women could be found standing on a platform once more, many other passengers and bomb wreckage all around, waiting for the train from Düsseldorf that would take Erika to the capital of the Reich, Berlin.

Soon the long and dirty train roared in to a halt, with brakes squealing and valves hissing. Erika did not have to go looking for a compartment with an unoccupied seat – there was one right in front of her.

'Always remember,' Erna repeated, 'you're not alone on this trip. The uniform is well and good, but what's much more important is that God is with you, and he will help you.' After one last hug she helped Erika climb aboard. Then she lifted the suitcase and bag into the train, and slammed the door.

'Thanks again for everything, Aunt Erna,' was all Erika managed to say. It was harder than she'd expected to say goodbye, even with the excitement of seeing her family again. As it happened she wasn't able to wave goodbye, as the seat nearest the door window was taken: a soldier was saying goodbye to his wife. So, drying her eyes, Erika screwed up her handkerchief and sat down on the one empty seat in the small compartment. She kept her eyes closed as a sign to the other passengers that she wanted to catch up on some sleep at this early hour.

She had no intention of sleeping, of course, but equally she didn't want to have to make conversation – least of all with any of the *Landser*, the soldiers who had joined her after helping her get her luggage onto the storage rack. So she began to think about meeting her mother again, and her sister and brothers. And she fretted about the journey ahead . . . the other people in the compartment, those that she would meet on other trains. It was a long way. The trip to Berlin alone would take ten hours, and that was if nothing unexpected occurred along the way. This looked like being one long, boring trip.

The journey certainly turned out to be long, but not boring. Erika soon came to a decision: she was not going to be some snivelling little girl who kept herself to herself because she was scared of other people. So, after she had actually dropped off to sleep for a while, she suddenly sat up straight, as if to announce: 'All right, everybody – here I am. Now you can talk to me if you want to.' And pretty soon all eight people were deep in conversation, asking each other where they came from and where they were going and why they were going there. Everyone wanted to go to Berlin, but some were going on further east. There was plenty to talk about, and even if the young Erika didn't know enough to join in all of the discussion, she listened and she learned.

What did she know about the People's Court in Nuremberg and its particularly fierce presiding judge Roland Freisler? Or the public trial and the sentences given to the traitors of the 20th July? What did she know about the Allies advancing on the Reich's western borders? Or the V2, this miraculous weapon that the scientist Wernher von Braun had invented, and which would hopefully – no, definitely – bring defeat to the enemy? She knew next to nothing of the news and comment in the *National Observer* or the *German Times*.

Even so, one topic pulled the ballerina into the discussion. One of the women had a *Berlin Illustrated Times* on her, which reported the closing down of the Scala and how the members of the ballet ensembles had had to take jobs in the defence industry. Erika told the others about her own training as a ballerina, and about the small dancing parts she had already managed to get. As she warmed to her subject she told them about Fanny Elssler, the famous Austrian dancer of the previous century, who was her role model. Sadly there wasn't enough space in the compartment to show the other travellers what she could do! She would have loved to show them some of the basic positions and steps, like the *arabesque, attitude, frappé*, or the *glissé* – even to turn a *pirouette*. But all she could do was describe each one with as many gestures and words as she could muster.

Everyone was delighted with it all, though so many new people boarded at Hannover and Magdeburg that conversation soon dried up again. Things now became so cramped that one of the soldiers offered to take Erika on his lap 'to make room'. Erika mounted a vigorous defence. 'I might be small,' she said, 'and light . . . but I'm not a child! I'm a member of the BDM; I don't just sit on any man's lap! I'd rather sit on my suitcase to make room!' Which she did, for the rest of the journey.

Late in the afternoon the train arrived at Berlin. Amid hundreds of people Erika had to change trains and find her way across the badly damaged station in Charlottenburg. Happily some of the soldiers from her compartment were after the same train. They had already proved themselves trustworthy, so Erika gladly went with them. They found some seats, but once again things were cramped, so again Erika sat on her suitcase . . . Sitting was definitely better than standing, even if it was uncomfortable: at just four foot ten in her shoes there was no way she'd have been able to reach the ceiling handles anyway.

This train would take them to Reppen, a junction to the east of Frankfurt-an-der-Oder. From there Erika could catch a train to Prussia. She hoped the train would be on time, and in fact there were few problems along the way, although sometimes the train would stop for no apparent reason, or it would drop to walking speed (getting out and picking flowers was not allowed!), and on one occasion the train simply stopped at an unannounced station. To Erika's disappointment the atmosphere in the compartment on this journey was dull – not nearly as cheerful as before. Maybe it had something to do with the SS officer standing in the corner, pressed to a window, with what surely was a sinister expression on his face.

There were no problems changing trains in Reppen, thanks again to the soldiers who were on their way back to their units in the Baltic states. There were fewer passengers headed for the north-east, so at last Erika had a seat to herself, even one at the window. Too bad, then, that it was pitch-black outside! Erika would have loved to see the countryside and villages in the Wartheland district, a region that had become Polish property in World War I and which the Führer had later annexed to the German Reich. Erika had been here several times before with her mother, and her mother had pointed out loads of things.

But now it was night. Maybe it would be better to use the time for sleep. She knew there was no need to be scared – these soldiers would do her no harm. They were a merry lot, especially Hein, the blond guy from Friesland. And they had made quite clear their respect for this young BDM girl who was willing to move to one of the eastern districts to play her part in the war effort.

As the sun rose, and Erika awoke, the train was already approaching the beautiful old Hanseatic city of Torun on the Weichsel, where over 400 years before the famous astronomer Nicolaus Copernicus had been born. Erika thought of school. On the other side of the River Weichsel was the Kulm area, and Gosslershausen, the home of Grandma Luise.

Erika thought about each one in turn: Grandma Luise, Mamá, Hellmuth, Hildegard, Siegfried. And then there was Grandpa Kiel as well. He was Grandma's third husband, not the children's actual grandfather, but they still called him Grandpa. He was a kind old gentleman, for some reason always called by his surname, Grandpa Kiel.

It took the train an hour and a half to cover the last forty miles. But the time was helped on its way by a cheerful atmosphere in the compartment, matched by the sunny autumn day outside. 'What are you going to do once you've arrived at Gosslershausen?' asked Hein from Friesland, who had noticed Erika's excitement.

'What am I going to do?'

'Well, I mean, you can't just get out and say "Here I am",' the soldier explained.

'And why's that?' Erika pressed.

'Well, your arrival is something special. So you have to do something special.'

'And what might that be?' Erika wondered where this was going; the others were following the conversation keenly.

'Well, I mean, you definitely can't use the normal exit off the train,' Hein said with a serious look on his face.

Erika was a little startled. 'Why not?'

'The door is blocked, *min Deern*.[3] There's no way you'll get out. We couldn't get the thing open back in Torun. Didn't you notice?'

'Nonsense, nobody got on or off in Torun. There was no need to open the door,' Erika replied.

'Well, the train'll soon be arriving at Hohenkirch. Then you can see for yourself. We can't exactly try while we're going at full speed.'

---

[3] 'my girl' in a local dialect

'Yes!' said Erika, more worried than she let on. 'We'll see then!' Was he kidding? His comrades were grinning as if they were in on some secret. Perhaps they had concocted this story while she'd been sleeping.

But when the train stopped in Hohenkirch a little later, sure enough the compartment door really wouldn't open. Or so it seemed. Now Erika was really worried. How was she going to get out of the train at the next stop, in just fifteen minutes' time?

'Don't you worry, *min Deern* – it's no problem. We'll help you. You'll soon be hugging your mother.'

The last fifteen minutes ticked by. Just after Hohenkirch Erika put on her coat and took her suitcase and bag. Finally they saw the small town, and the train pulled into the station with the usual squeal of brakes.

'And now?' she asked, looking at the soldier expectantly.

'Well, there's a window in the door. We'll just lift you through it. Shouldn't be a problem with a featherweight like you,' Hein responded, already winding down the window. He leaned out and shouted: 'Hello, Grandma Luise! And grandchildren! Here comes your Erika!' Then he called to one of the rail guards standing on the platform: 'Would you take this *Deern*, please? She needs to get off here, but the door won't open.' At this he lifted Erika up by her waist and handed her through the open window.

Erika was laughing. As soon as she was let down she hugged her grandma, a woman no taller than Erika but considerably rounder. But then she started as the guard lifted his signalling disc and blew his whistle to tell the train to depart. The train driver's answering whistle sounded like a whale.

'My luggage! Where's my luggage?'

'Don't worry, *min Deern*,' Hein reassured her. He had meanwhile left the train . . . through the open compartment door.

'Here's your luggage. Have a great time with your family, and working in West Prussia. Take care, *min Deern*, and *Heil Hitler!*'

Before Erika could say a thing the young soldier had already reboarded the train, now slowly pulling away. 'Oh, that crook!' Erika laughed. 'The door wasn't jammed at all! Those tricksters . . .' She waved at them and called out, 'Courage always against the enemy! *Heil Hitler!*' And then she turned to greet Grandma Luise and her family properly. Hellmuth had skipped school to come and welcome his big sister.

Mamá wasn't there. Grandma addressed Erika's thoughts before she even found the words. 'You'll see your mother tonight. She's at work on the railways.'

'It's great you're all here to meet me!' said Erika happily.

'It's great you're here!' her brothers and sister replied, and the two youngest began to bombard her with this and that. Grandma cut in, 'Your sister's hardly got here! There'll be time enough to talk. I expect Erika's very tired.'

'More hungry than tired, Grandma. And I wouldn't mind some water either. My bag and my bottle have been empty for a long time.'

'Soon, soon. At home I've got some lovely stew waiting for you. Grandpa's keeping it warm on the fire. And we've got some delicious elderberry juice.'

'Oh, you didn't make pea soup, Grandma, did you?' Erika frowned. 'You know I don't like pea soup.'

'Don't worry. There are no peas in the soup! But we've got loads of other vegetables – even meat.'

Siegfried piped up: 'Grandpa Kiel even killed a chicken, specially for the home-coming stew!'

Then Hildegard chimed in: 'It was so gross when he cut off the chicken's head! Ugh!' She shuddered at the memory. 'I ran away!'

Fortunately there was a wooden wheelbarrow at the front of the station. This meant they didn't have to carry Erika's bag and suitcase on the long walk to Dietrichsdorf. Hellmuth knew how to handle this one-wheeled vehicle perfectly – even with his little sister or brother sitting on top of it.

It was a long way through the village. Jabtonowo had a predominantly Polish population. The streets had an air of neglect. Recent rain had left large puddles in the uneven cobblestones and in the sandy tracks they came to after that. The houses and shacks along the street looked quite run down, somehow still gloomy despite the radiant glow of the autumn sun on the leaves of the trees.

The few people they saw seemed just as destitute. Not even the children seemed very happy. The main sounds they heard were made by the hosts of chickens roaming the streets. Along with ducks and geese they flocked at every house, scratching, clucking and quacking. And then there were the cats and dogs. Every other house seemed to have a yapping mongrel. Erika did not like dogs. Happily these were all chained up or behind a fence.

'Be careful – don't let this gander get you,' warned Grandma Luise when they approached the busy village pond. 'He's evil. And he doesn't like Germans.'

'As if a bird could tell who's Polish and who's German!' Erika retorted.

'He seems to know! He probably learned it from his owners. They don't like Germans either.'

'So how do you all get on with each other?' Erika was curious to know.

'Oh, it works pretty well for the most part. You see one person and avoid the next. It's as simple as that. Germans keep to themselves, Poles keep to themselves . . .'

'How about where you live? Aren't there just a few houses there, but quite a few Poles?'

'No, we don't have any problems. Everybody works through each day and minds their own business. If one of us needs help, we ask someone of our own nationality. That's how we avoid trouble.'

'But Grandma, Polish people are human beings too!'

'Of course, they're human beings all right . . . but they're dirty and lazy – completely different from Germans. If this area had stayed German back in 1920, I'm sure things would look very different here . . . so much cleaner and tidier. But now we have to live – and fight – in Polish conditions.'

As they walked home the two women had to take a particularly muddy road. The children had run ahead of them with the wheelbarrow, deftly steering it around the muddy potholes. They had passed the geese with their wild chief undisturbed. 'You haven't got a pair of rubber boots I could wear, Grandma?' Erika asked. 'This mud's ruining my best shoes!'

'I have,' Grandma assured her. 'But I'm afraid this is what you get here. When it rains heavily most of the roads turn to mud instantly. I blame the Polish council. So far, five years of German administration haven't changed much. But it will . . . eventually. It'll take time, and more German labour.'

'I'm sure it'll get better once this war is over,' Erika sighed.

'Ah, once this war is over . . .' her grandma replied in a curious tone of voice.

'You don't sound very confident,' Erika said, as she negotiated yet another large muddy puddle.

'You don't think so? Ha, your mother's still convinced Hitler will win in the end. I'm not so sure any more. There's too much talk about loss of life and materials, about the fronts crumbling, and withdrawal, and giving ground. They say the Russians have already reached Warsaw and the Czech border, and some are even harassing our troops in the Baltic states now. That's not good news for us here.'

'You think the Russians will get this far?' Erika replied with amazement.

'How do I know? Let's hope not. I'm sure our brave boys will know how to stop them.'

'But not the handful of men that we saw in the village just now, Grandma,' Erika said doubtfully.

'I suppose not . . . you may be right, Erika. But let's change the subject. We're almost there. And Grandpa's waiting with that stew.'

The cottage had a large living room which doubled as a kitchen. It was already dark when Greta returned from work, and the room was lit by two carbide lamps. Grandma and her grandchildren were sitting at the table, all chatting away happily. Grandpa Kiel had given Erika a hearty welcome and had already gone to bed. He said he was feeling his eighty years.

As soon as her mother came in Erika leapt from her chair and shouted, 'Mamá, here I am!' Running round the table, she flung her arms around her neck.

Greta stiffened, just about tolerating the outburst. It seemed that French form of address was still bothering her . . . 'So you're finally here. About time too. Hopefully not messed up by Aunt Erna. And I am your *mother*,' she said rather harshly.

Erika struggled with the cold welcome. 'What do you mean, *Mother*, not messed up by Aunt Erna?'

'All right, all right. I see you're still wearing your uniform . . . you don't seem to have been totally contaminated by her religion.' And that was that. Suddenly Greta was asking for something to eat. She was back in her routine, as if this was a day like any other, as if her daughter's arrival after months apart was nothing out of the ordinary. No questions about those past months, or what sort of journey she'd had, or how Aunt Erna was doing. Erika felt more like a servant than a daughter.

What was going on? Did she really annoy her mother that much when she called her *Mamá*? She'd said it without thinking, in the joy of the moment. Perhaps Greta had had a bad day at work. Or bad news? There was no *People's Receiver* or other newspaper in the house. Or was her basic grievance with the local Polish government?

Or was she afraid that her daughter had got religion?

Right now Erika wasn't going to figure out her mother's behaviour, so she decided to suppress her disappointment, and to serve her mother as though they'd not been separated all this time. But nothing changed, and the remainder of the meal time was spent in silence. Even Siegfried and Hildegard had stopped their chattering. Something was clearly wrong, so Erika decided to keep herself to herself, at least when her mother was at home.

As they finished dinner Greta announced, 'From now on, due to Grandma's and Grandpa's age, you are the official helper in this household, Erika. Quite apart from my job I have to take care of the few German women in the village. These are hard times, and they're going to get harder.' She turned towards Grandma and continued: 'It will be easier for you now, Mother. Don't hesitate to give your granddaughter enough work, so that you've got all the time you need for Grandpa. I'm tired, so I'm off to bed now. Goodnight. Germany, *Sieg Heil!*'

When she'd gone Erika threw her grandma a puzzled look in the dim light. Grandma indicated with a look and a slight nod that Erika was not to react. Later on, all she would say was that Erika's mother had changed a lot lately, becoming more and more fanatical in her views on National Socialism. She wouldn't tolerate any doubt about Hitler's Final Victory claims. And if Hitler's mission should actually fail . . . there was no telling how Greta would react.

Erika got her brothers and sister ready for sleep. Her two brothers shared a bed, with one pillow and one blanket between them. Erika herself would be sharing the shallow crate that was Hildegard's bed, once she had finished tidying the living room. The room was tiny, and besides the two beds there was only room for a small trunk. The only window was so small not even the moonlight seemed to get through. Still, she was home with her family. Now at last she sang their favourite song: 'Heidschi, Bumbeidschi . . . .'

The whole family had to wash in a big bowl in the kitchen part of the living room. The little ones went first. Water was fetched from the well in the courtyard and taken out again when they were done. Towels and wet clothes were dried on a metal bar at the stove, or on a washing line above it. To go to the toilet they had to walk across the courtyard to a tiny hut next to a weather-beaten wooden shed, with a small heart-shaped opening in the door that supplied natural air-conditioning . . . There was no lid on the hole, but there were strips of newspaper on a nail. The printer's ink came off easily . . . even in the extreme winter cold.

What a decline in living standards, Erika thought as she snuggled up to her little sister who was snoring gently in her sleep. All this for Reich and Führer! Was the sacrifice really worth it? Would the day come when Adolf Hitler appreciated all the sacrifices that his subjects had freely made for the fatherland? Probably best not think of what was to come . . . She closed her eyes and soon fell into a deep sleep.

As the days went by Erika got used to her new living and working conditions. It was different from the other times she had been here as a visitor. In those days she was always going back to a real house with glass windows, with doors that could be locked, a real bathroom and a zinc bath. And a bed of her own.

But here . . . broken windows were stuffed with old rags – no one to mend the windows, of course. The front door was warped and hard to close – no carpenter or locksmith to come and have a look at it. Grandpa Kiel was too frail. There was no bath at all, not even a wooden one to carry into the living room. If you wanted a bath, you could have one in the lake nearby, or in the River Ossa. But only during the summer.

In Gosslershausen there was a little shop, but the items on sale didn't compare to those you could still buy in the Ruhr, even in wartime. 'Settling here to spread our German customs is our second sacrifice for Führer and fatherland. Get used to it!' So said Greta, and no way was Erika to argue. 'This will all look very different in a few years from now,' Greta assured her, although just how that was going to happen she couldn't say.

Erika had no choice but to accept her new circumstances. Harder to accept was the fact that, with each passing day and week she spent here, her ballet career was floating away . . . like the twig she now watched gliding down the Ossa. Would she ever wear her tutu again, put on her ballet shoes, dance the *corps de ballet* or *pas de deux*? She could sense that her dream would never come true and, when her mother was not around, she wept.

Greta's opinion was quite clear: what the Reich needed was women of experience to bear children and to work – not girls who only lived for the amusement of others.

Grandma Luise had more sympathy for the silent pain of her grandchild. Not that she could really console Erika – she herself had been having bad feelings about the future for a long time. Naturally she thought better of sharing these with her daughter: Greta would just make a fuss about her mother's illicit doubts.

Luise was happy to see that the three younger ones had no problems with the conditions here, either at home or in the village. Nor did they seem particularly worried about the uncertain future. They lived each day quite carefree, enjoying their games indoors and out, sometimes getting into trouble for the tricks they played on man and beast. Erika was the most frequent victim of their pranks: they knew she couldn't stand spiders or mice. And whenever Felix did what cats do, and brought a new find into the house, Erika would find the unfortunate deceased on her chair, beside her plate, or under her blanket.

They did the same thing with the spiders. Grandma Luise and Grandpa Kiel were actually quite amused when their 'official assistant' got all het up about the little fellows. 'Silly poppet, why get worked up over such trifles?' Her grandma's expression reminded Erika of when she had been a child herself, scared of dead creatures even then. Yet still somehow she couldn't overcome her fear.

But for now, this was the worst Erika had to contend with. Life together in the cottage worked out well enough, not least because the war didn't really touch them directly.

But elsewhere, the war raged on.

October 1944 was spent working in the garden and fields. Potatoes and beets had to be dug up, other vegetables had to be gathered, and the garden had to be prepared for the long winter. There was plenty of work to do. Even the little ones had to knuckle down now. They had to help prepare various shrubs and trees for the winter. Grandpa Kiel would tell them what to do, and Grandma Luise gave what help she could. It was arduous work for Erika, who was not used to it, nor exactly strong either. But her grandparents were satisfied with her work. If only Greta would say something encouraging or appreciative. But it was as if this level of commitment was only to be expected of a true German girl. Other girls probably had to cope with harsher conditions, and live away from their families. So Erika had better be grateful!

She was. But she looked forward to the days when the work outside would be finished and all her work would be indoors. Those days came sooner than expected. Erika had just celebrated her eighteenth birthday on the 21st November when winter arrived. Within a couple of days the country was covered by a thick, white blanket. The cold came from the north-east, bringing with it not only snow, but events which would have terrifying effects on the land and its people.

CHAPTER 3

The Russians Are Coming!

With the snows came the news that Soviet troops had forced their way into East Prussia, wreaking havoc. It was said they were like animals, plundering, raping and murdering without pity. But German troops were now driving the barbarians further east. As Greta told them the news, clearly excited, Erika felt a shiver run down her spine. What if the Russians made their way further south-east, and the German troops failed to stop them? What if the soldiers reached their village? According to Grandma, they had come within 150 miles. Erika couldn't bear to think about it. Greta said it wouldn't happen . . .

Erika decided to plan ahead. She needed a place to hide, just in case, where somebody might be able to bring her food. It would have to be somewhere in the village where the Russians wouldn't look. They'd probably search the houses, sheds and barns that belonged to the German population. But maybe they'd leave the Polish people alone. So a barn belonging to a Polish farmer might be a safe hiding place.

Erika knew of such a barn on the Budziks' farm, which was at the edge of the village. It lay some way away from the street and the railway line. Erika got on well with Jarek and Jagoda Budzik. Somehow these two elderly people weren't exactly Polish – they even spoke German quite well. Yes, she would try to find a place to hide there.

She decided against telling the family her plans. Grandma Luise and Grandpa Kiel were old and presented no threat to the Russians. They would be spared. Hellmuth, Hildegard and Siegfried were children, so they should be safe. Her mother would know how to defend herself if anyone tried anything. But as a young woman Erika would definitely be at risk.

She decided to pay the farm a visit. The old couple were sympathetic to her fears, and together they prepared a hiding place in the barn. At the back there were some big straw bales which they rearranged to make a hiding place. The bales let enough air through, and one of them could easily be rolled away so Erika could get in and out.

The couple said they'd make sure she didn't die of hunger or thirst, but one thing she would have to endure was permanent darkness. But even so she would find refuge in this place, they said kindly – and a lot of time for prayer. They suggested Erika ask Mary and all the saints to help her.

Pray? Erika was surprised how this suggestion took hold of her thinking during the days that followed. Religion hadn't been an issue since she'd arrived at Gosslershausen, and old ideas had re-established themselves in her mind, not least that a German girl doesn't pray! And anyway, who would she pray to? Mary and the saints? Hardly! That was Catholic – this much the Protestant Erika knew. To God, then? But which god? She had attended confirmation classes several years ago, but she'd not found God there. To Providence perhaps? But what was this Providence

Hitler was always going on about, and which clearly meant so much to her mother?

Erika thought about Aunt Erna again. Now *she* knew her God. She had shown Erika how to trust in God and how to pray to the 'one true God' who had created everything and sent his Son into the world so that humanity could be saved. Soon it would be Christmas . . . wasn't this Son of God, Jesus, supposed to be at the heart of Christmas?

Erika mulled it all over. 'Why don't you just try it?' she asked herself. And once more she recalled her confirmation verse:

> The Lord is with me; I will not be afraid.
> What can man do to me?
> The Lord is with me; he is my helper.[1]

The Lord? Now this was God, the one the Bible talked about and Aunt Erna believed in, who had sent his Son. Why not really pray to him? If the Russians came, there'd be plenty of opportunity to test whether these verses were true!

None of the family noticed Erika's secret preparations. Her mother was out at work on the railways during the day. When she returned in the evenings she would tell them the latest news – news which, as a devout follower of the Führer, she liked less each day. She simply couldn't understand why Hitler had left his East Prussian headquarters, the so-called 'Wolf Redoubt', back in November.

Greta remained in denial over the presence of Soviet troops in East Prussia until the day all train services were terminated and she lost her job at the State Railway. She knew there had to be a

---

[1] Psalm 118:6–7

reason for that. And there had to be a reason why more and more German farmers were leaving the country. Despite the harsh winter they could be seen passing through the village with their horses and wagons, heading west. By Christmas several families from Gosslershausen itself had left with their horses and wagons packed high, abandoning house and farm to the remaining Polish population.

'Wimps! They're a load of cowards! Traitors to the Reich!' was Greta's response. 'They're not true Germans.' But Grandma's advice was to leave with the children and join one of the refugee trains herself. Grandpa Kiel joined in: 'If Luise and I were still young, we wouldn't sacrifice ourselves to the Russians here, Greta. We'd leave before it was too late.'

'Enough, Grandpa, be quiet!' Greta's fury did not relent. 'I'm not listening to this!'

'You have a responsibility to your children,' the old man retorted.

'And to the Reich! What's going to happen here if everybody runs away?'

'Nothing's going to happen here, Greta,' Grandma said. 'Think of the children, and leave with the rest.'

'My children are German children, and we're staying! Now, I'll hear no more about it!' Greta's tone brought the argument to an end. In the darkened room she couldn't see her elderly parents shaking their heads, or the tears running down her mother's cheeks, or the fearful eyes in the pale faces of her children.

Nor could she see the defiance etched in her daughter's face. If Erika really did have to stay, then it was just as well she'd planned ahead. Her mother wouldn't have to worry about her when danger came.

In the middle of January 1945 the first Soviet troops were unmistakably in evidence – you couldn't miss the remote thunder of their guns, just a few miles away to the south-east.

The German military wanted to ensure the Russians found no village when they finally arrived, so the people that remained were gathered together, Germans and Polish alike, in the village square, in front of the house of the local military commander. He was a strict-looking officer, dressed in black from head to toe, and he told the small crowd of elderly men and women, plus children, all wrapped in their thick winter clothes, that they had four hours to pack their most important things. The village was to be surrendered – they would be setting the farms and cottages on fire, leaving nothing of value for the Russians. 'There are no exceptions – not even Polish properties,' he barked. 'This is an irrevocable order of the local district government. If anyone is left in any of the houses after the deadline, their safety cannot be guaranteed.'

There was a moment of shocked silence and then a wave of protest. Unperturbed by the soldiers positioned behind the officer, they complained that it couldn't possibly be the will of district headquarters, or the Führer, to treat them like this . . . to simply destroy German property and burn the land. And it made no sense to deport the Polish population. Where were they supposed to go? They'd hardly be welcome in the West. If Polish territory was in Russian hands already, they may as well stay put. The German and Polish communities in the village didn't exactly like each other, but they'd always managed to get on with each other.

Erika watched the whole scene as she held on to her sister and brothers, the tension growing inside her all the while. At this point Grandpa Kiel and Jarek Budzik stepped forward as spokesmen of the two ethnic groups, and began to negotiate with the officer in black. They made it clear that no one was about to just get up and abandon their property. If they were really going to set light to the farms, then everyone would be burned. This was now a matter for local government, or the armed forces, not least the madman who had given the order in the first place.

As the man in black listened his face grew bright red. Then he pulled himself up to his full height and, with a voice that trembled with anger, said, 'I have informed you of the order from Local HQ. Whoever refuses to comply is liable for the consequences. *Heil Hitler!*' With that he turned on the heels of his shiny polished boots, went to the house of the local military commander, and ordered the small troop to follow him in.

The townspeople continued to talk for a while, reaffirming their intention not to leave their homes and farms. Slowly they began to disperse, some of them in silence, others in heated debate.

As they walked back to Dietrichsdorf Grandma Luise asked Greta once more if she wouldn't take the children. Greta cut her off. 'Be quiet, Mother, I'm staying! They won't burn down the village!'

Erika shivered. She had made up her mind. As she passed the Budziks she whispered, 'As soon as the Russians are here I'll come over.'

Greta proved to be right. After only one hour the unnamed officer in black left Gosslershausen along with his soldiers. They drove off quickly, disappearing in a whirl of snow. The village had been officially surrendered and – along with its residents – left to its fate. But at least it was still standing.

No one else left. They all waited anxiously, listening night and day for strange sounds that must come from the south-east. Yet in the meantime they got on with their winter domestic chores. There were animals to be fed – poultry, cattle, pigs – it didn't seem right that any of these should suffer just because their owners were running for their lives.

And that's how things were on the 21st January. Shortly after sunrise Greta was running over to a deserted farm to feed the cow and do the milking. Erika was doing her usual morning housework. Grandpa Kiel was sitting at his customary place in the window, exchanging some words with his wife now and then between naps. Grandma Luise was reading something to her grandchildren. And suddenly there it was – the thunder of guns outside, with shells exploding and machine guns rattling.

'They're coming,' Grandma Luise whispered simply. She grimaced, and lowered the book into her lap. Erika gave a shriek and dropped an earthenware jug which broke into a thousand pieces. So this was it. Time to make her discreet withdrawal.

A few moments after the first wave of explosions, Greta came running into the room. 'They're outside the village,' she said quietly. 'Those shots were just an announcement. They'll be here any minute. Now we show them the spirit of a true German.'

Fine. Go ahead and show them your spirit, Erika thought, as she waited for a moment when she could leave the room unnoticed. Her chance came when her mother sat at the table and covered her face with her hands as she let out a sigh. The three little ones gathered around her. Erika left the room quickly and put on her winter shoes in the hallway. She grabbed her warm winter coat, together with her scarf, cap, gloves and a large shawl, and crept quietly out of the house and away from the farm, avoiding the view from the living room. She heard her mother call her name. 'May God protect you all in there,' she thought.

Erika was gone, on a mission to save her life. She was determined not to become some Russian soldier's helpless victim. Within minutes she was sitting in her hiding place in the barn, wrapped in her warm clothes, plus an extra woollen blanket which Jagoda Budzik had handed to her. Yet still it was cold, very cold. She shivered, as much from anxiety as from the freezing conditions. How long would she have to sit here, waiting for the danger to pass? What was going on in the village? What did those sporadic explosions and muffled shots mean? What was her family thinking about her now? Could they do anything to protect themselves?

And where was her father? She had not heard anything from him for so long!

All these thoughts running through her mind made her feel dizzy and sick. Then she heard the sound of somebody coming up to the barn. But it was only Jarek and Jagoda, bringing food and drink to their secret guest.

'Everything okay in there? Russians at other end of village. Will for sure come back later. Must not forget to pray, Erika. *Z'Bogiem*. We go again.'

That was Jagoda's voice. Jarek had handed her a piece of bread and a bottle of hot tea through the opening in the straw. He repeated the *Z'Bogiem* and then the two of them left.

Z'Bogiem. Erika knew that meant 'Goodbye' in the full sense of 'God be with you'. The Polish often said it to each other when they were parting. She wondered whether God was really here with her in her cave of straw. And was he with her family? They knew less about God than she did. Perhaps he was with Grandma Luise and Grandpa Kiel? Did they already know him? They'd never talked about him . . . Erika's mother would never have allowed them to . . . but then they didn't mention anything about God even when Greta was out.

Erika reflected on her decision a couple of days earlier to pray for God's protection when danger came. So in the darkness of her straw hidey-hole she tried to tell God – though she didn't really know him – what was on her mind. She remembered Aunt Erna explaining to her that she could talk to God just as she would to someone sitting next to her. So Erika concentrated her thoughts on what was worrying her, as she sat alone in the darkness of her self-imposed dungeon. She thought of the cold, the darkness, and her sadness over her loved ones who didn't know where she was. She faced her fear that the Russians might find her, and punish her for hiding . . . maybe even rape her. 'No, God, please no. Don't let them violate me. Please, God, not that.'

She had spoken these last words out loud, and she was startled when, just at that moment, loud voices approached the barn. They didn't sound German or Polish. Erika tried to make herself small and held her breath. She sent up a silent prayer: 'God, help me now!'

The voices grew louder. They were Russian. She could hear Jarek assuring them over and over again that there were no Germans in his barn. Erika knew the word for Germans, *Niemiec.* Suddenly they were inside and what she assumed were bayonets came poking through the straw. Eventually they gave up and left, talking loudly with each other the whole time. It didn't sound very friendly. Finally it grew quiet.

Erika let out a sigh of relief. Maybe God *had* helped in this first Russian attack! Her hiding place was secure, for now – though she knew she would have to keep waiting, keep hoping, keep praying.

A while later her two Polish hosts came back to tell her it was evening and all was quiet. Erika asked them if they would go and tell her mother she was safe. She didn't want her family worrying about her all night. Jarek agreed, and soon she was alone again.

It must have been morning. Erika was woken by the sound of shots being fired somewhere on the farm. A second visit from the Russians? It was exactly as the day before. Were they even the same men? Erika didn't recognise their voices; all she could hear was Jarek with them in the barn again. The result was the same as the previous day too. Once more they went away empty-handed; once more she breathed a sigh of relief.

Had God helped her again? Possibly, even probably – but she didn't know for sure. All she could do, still, was hope, wait and pray. Later on Jagoda came in, opened the secret entrance to her prison, and handed her another piece of bread, with a slice of sausage and a refilled bottle.

'Is it all clear out there?' Erika asked. 'I need to go . . . desperately!'

'All clear. You come out,' the old lady replied. Erika crawled out of the straw hole and immediately disappeared behind the barn. After a few minutes she returned, still rearranging her clothes. 'That's better,' she said with evident relief. 'Does Mamá know . . .?'

'She know. She say it all right, *dobrze*. But terrible thing happened.'

'What happened?' Erika tensed.

'Russians and Grandpa Kiel . . .' The old Polish woman hesitated. Evidently she wasn't keen to say what happened.

'What did they do?' Erika pressed.

'Russian hit Grandpa Kiel in face with *karabin* . . . He barely alive.'

Erika groaned. 'Did they shoot him?'

'*Nie*, hit only . . . badly hit.'

'Oh, poor Grandpa Kiel. How is he now?'

'Is not dead. But barely alive.' Then Jagoda explained: 'Did not want to give watch.'

'And the others, Mamá, Hellmuth, Hildegard, Siegfried, Grandma?'

'They all are *in domu*, indoors. Mama been to commander but now come back. Grandpa hardly alive.'

'Wouldn't it be better if I went back home . . .?' Erika's question was directed at herself more than the old woman.

'*Nie*, better here in *stodola*, *prosze*, please. And not forget to pray.'

'What about the other people in the village?' Erika asked.

'Some people dead. Some shot – some by themselves. Some women gone.'

Erika was visibly shocked, and decided to take the woman's advice and return to her hiding place. Jagoda closed it from the outside. Erika was alone again in the dark, with just the thoughts of a heavy heart over what might be going on at home and in the village. And as she considered the whole situation, and what had happened to Grandpa Kiel, she realised that the Russians were eventually going to find her there – if not those who were in the village at the moment, then others who'd be bound to come after. Hiding wouldn't be an option for much longer. And anyway, she was putting the Budziks at risk. Better to go home rather than spend another night in the barn . . . Or should she wait a bit longer? Her thoughts began to torment her so severely she started to cry. She let the tears come. And, as she wept, she remembered.

Jagoda had told her not to forget to pray. 'So pray, Erika,' she told herself, as she wiped the tears from her eyes with her shawl and put her hands together.

She must have fallen asleep while she was praying. When she awoke the darkness had gone. Her shelter had been opened up. Three huge Russian soldiers were standing in front of the opening, aiming their guns right at her. Horrified, she shouted:

'No! Don't shoot! Please don't!' She tried to jump up but, short though she was, her head hit the straw bale above her. She slumped back to the ground and remained huddled in what was left of her hiding place. 'Just wait and see what they do,' she thought, and hid her face behind her arms. She felt strangely calm.

The three Russians said nothing but just grinned at each other and at the girl in front of them. The situation seemed to amuse them. They clearly seemed to know that someone had been hiding in the barn. There was no sign of Jarek or Jagoda. Had they been taken away for giving shelter to a German? Or did they even know that three Russians had forced their way into the barn and found her?

The weirdest thoughts were running through her head. What was she actually waiting for here all huddled up? For one of them to pull the trigger, or stab her with a bayonet? Or would one of them – all of them – fall upon her? Fearfully, Erika looked up between her arms and saw that one of the men was bending down and offering her his free hand. He wanted to help her get up. He said something that might have meant 'Come on'. Erika took his hand and let him pull her up, and then she beat the dust from her clothes.

Now what? The young man, wrapped in a winter coat and shawl, looked expectantly at the other men, as if to ask 'What now?'

The men no longer looked like dangerous giants to Erika, even though they were much taller than her. One of them indicated by nodding his head and gesturing with his hand that she was to walk in front of them out of the barn. He had shouldered his gun, and his comrades now did the same. Clearly they had decided she represented no threat, and didn't look like she was about to make a run for it. After several minutes they reached their local headquarters, set up in the very same building that the German soldiers had left only a couple of days before.

They had not met a single person on the way. Erika wondered what had happened to them. Had they run off scared and hidden somewhere? Or maybe the snow, which swallowed all sound, had laid a blanket of silence over everything. Even now she could hardly hear the voices of the three soldiers talking behind her. And she could only guess what they were talking about.

Inside the house Erika faced an elderly officer. He addressed her in a friendly manner, speaking almost perfect German. 'Well, little lady. Didn't work out with the hiding place, did it? Our people find everybody.'

Erika just shrugged. She wanted to avoid saying the wrong thing. She sent up a quick prayer. For a second the thought crossed her mind that God really was with her, right now, and that he would help her to do the right thing.

Then the interrogation began. 'What is your name? How old are you? Where do you live? Where is your mother? Where is your father? Do you have brothers and sisters? Other relatives? Where do they live and what do they do? Do you have a job? Do you belong to Hitler Youth? What do you think of Adolf Hitler and the war?'

The 'little lady' must answer everything honestly. 'No lies, no wrong answers,' the officer kept saying. Erika complied, answering every question, even the ones about her attitude to the German Reich and its great Führer. She wanted the Russians to know that she'd had no other choice as a young woman than to join the BDM, and that she would have preferred to finish her training as a dancer in Dortmund than to live in this village far away from her real home.

Erika could see that the man behind the desk was impressed by her openness, possibly even amused by it. But why pretend? He translated some of her answers for the others in the room. They seemed to share his amusement.

Finally, the man had asked enough questions. He put his pen on the desk and said: 'You can go home, little lady. But do not leave the village. We still need you.'

Whatever he had meant by this remark, Erika was relieved she was allowed to go. She tightened her coat around her and tied her belt, put her cap and gloves on again, took her shawl under her arm, and left the building like someone who'd just won an unequal fight. She had survived her first interrogation by the Soviet soldiers without harm. This seemed to her a small miracle, one that only God could have done. That speedy prayer had been answered. God had been with her and helped her.

Erika could not have known just then how many more prayers like this she'd be sending up. She was simply glad that she'd been treated with mercy and could go home unmolested.

A strange sense of elation swept over her as she trudged through the fresh snow towards Dietrichsdorf. She thought about Mamá, the children, Grandma and Grandpa, and began to worry about what she would find there. When she finally got home she found the whole family gathered in the living room around Grandpa Kiel's deathbed. In fact the dear old man had died the previous night from the injuries he'd sustained because he refused to give his watch to a Russian soldier.

Greta stood up with some difficulty to greet her daughter, but this time she wasted no time in giving her a hug. 'Are you all right?' she whispered. 'Did they do anything to you?'

'I'm fine, thank God,' Erika said. 'They were friendly to me. And they said they still needed me.'

Tears filled her eyes. 'Poor Grandpa Kiel.' Swallowing hard, she stood at the bed and looked at her grandfather. Half of his face was covered – presumably the side that had received the fatal blow.

'Those pigs killed him . . .' Grandma sobbed; 'killed a defenceless old man because of a watch.' She stroked her husband's cold cheek. The three little ones were sitting pale-faced and in silence at the other end of the bier. So young to have to face such an inhuman death up close, thought Erika, who had not experienced such a thing herself as yet.

After a few moments she asked: 'And what is going to happen with Grandpa Kiel now?'

Her mother gave a sigh: 'We must bury him with the others.'

'What others?' Erika started.

'The ones killed by those barbarians.'

'And the ones who . . . themselves . . .' Erika fumbled a reply.

'How do you know about this?'

'Jagoda told me. She also told me about Grandpa Kiel.'

'They were behaving like pigs in the village. Some of the women preferred death to rape.'

Erika looked at her mother with wide eyes. 'And you?'

'They were satisfied with what they did to Grandpa. Or maybe your brothers and sister saved me.'

'Were the little ones there?'

'I'm afraid so. We were all in the living room.'

'But why didn't Grandpa Kiel just give them the watch?'

'I don't know, Erika. But maybe he saved us from worse.'

'Will the Russians come back?'

'Oh, there'll be more. Whole armies are on their way, destroying the land and the people. The battle is lost. Hitler has failed. Poor, wretched Germany.'

'Mamá, what are you saying? From your own lips!'

Her mother did not react. She was already thinking ahead. 'Get your suitcase. That way it's already packed when they get here.' Then, from the top of a cupboard, she grabbed a small item wrapped in paper. 'If they try to get at you, use this blade. You know what I mean. A German girl will not be taken by a Russian rat. Put it in your skirt pocket, so it's always handy.'

Erika's eyes grew wider. Her mother had changed a lot in these few days.

'Now, off you go and pack. You don't know when they'll come for you.'

Anxiously Erika did as she was told, though her mother's last words frightened her. What if the Russians took her with them and weren't so friendly this time? And could she really use a knife? 'A German girl will not be taken. . .' Surely God could spare her this.

Erika wanted to live. Surely Adolf Hitler, the 'greatest strategist of all time', had to see that victory was now impossible. Why didn't he surrender? The deployment of Russian troops at the eastern front had turned out to be anything but the 'bluff' that Hitler had called it. They were here, and more to follow. Soon they'd be in Berlin, and then . . .

Erika pulled her suitcase out from under her bed and began to pack what she thought she might need. She could not begin to imagine what lay ahead.

In the afternoon of the same day, two rather nervous-looking young Russians came to the house – they stayed at the garden gate, brandishing their guns to make sure nobody came near. With them they had a document which said that Miss Erika Remplin was to be at the house of the commandant at ten o'clock the next morning. Winter clothes were required, and light luggage was permitted.

If she failed to appear, the consequences for the family would be harsh.

CHAPTER 4

Deported

The letter caused various outbursts of panic throughout the house. Grandma started moaning about the 'cruel times we live in'. Hildegard started to cry for her sister, her tiny frame racked with sobs. Her two brothers remained silent, standing upright and completely motionless in a corner of the room. Greta was noticeably quiet, staring incessantly at the letter in her hand. No objection, no comment, no emotion. She sat down at Grandpa Kiel's bier and stared vacantly at nothing. The terrible events of the last few days had clearly worn her out, and now she wore disappointment like a shroud, her commitment to the Führer in shreds, and her deepest convictions shattered at the demise of National Socialist ideas. She was paralysed.

Erika herself seemed to be the calmest of all, even though she could not imagine what this letter meant for her. This much she did know: winter clothes and light luggage meant she was going on a journey. The route and the destination were unknown, and who could say whether she would ever come back?

Why was she so calm? Erika answered her own question immediately: she knew she was not alone. God was going to be

with her on this journey. He would help her as he had done over
the past few days.

> The Lord is with me; I will not be afraid.
>   What can man do to me?
> The Lord is with me; he is my helper.[1]

Yes, the Lord would be at her side, in all places and in all situations.
She had no idea where this confidence came from. It was just there.
And so, on the eve of her departure for nowhere, Erika was the only
one in the house who went to bed as normal.

Before they went to sleep she read another story to her sister
and brothers and sang their bedtime song to them. Without
thinking she changed the fourth verse:

> Heidschi Bumbeidschi, now come along,
> Come carry this maiden away from her home.
> I bid her good night, though she never return.
> Heidschi Bumbeidschi, boom-diddy-boom,
> Heidschi Bumbeidschi, boom-diddy-boom.

After the song she hugged all three of them one more time, and
snuggled up next to Hildegard. She wept silently, dwelling on
those words 'though she never return', and eventually fell asleep.

While she slept, Luise and Greta spent the night at Grandpa
Kiel's side, unable to sleep. They knew he'd not had long to live,
but to die in such a cruel way . . . And now Erika's enforced
home-leaving seemed even worse. They had no idea where she
was going, and could only guess what those Soviet monsters
would do with a young woman like her.

---

[1] Psalm 118:6–7

Would they ever meet again? Or find a grave where they could lay flowers? What a terrible thought! Why did it have to be like this? Greta could not begin to appreciate that many of the atrocities done by the enemy were nothing more than revenge, the same things the Germans had done in innumerable villages in the east. She probably didn't even know about most of it. All she knew was the nationalist propaganda that portrayed the enemy as capable of all kinds of atrocities, while her own people's actions went without comment.

Fear for Erika's future joined with many other thoughts to keep the two elderly women from sleep. When Erika came into the living room the next morning, dressed and almost ready to leave, she found them still sitting beside the body. Worn out by all the emotion, they had finally fallen asleep.

The room was already filled with the light of a wintry dawn. 'I'll prepare something to eat for the journey and then I'll go.' Erika's words brought the two women back to reality. They woke with a start and leapt to their feet.

'I'll do it!', they chorused, and soon both women got to work at the table, while Erika sat down and joined Grandpa Kiel as he waited quietly to be put into his grave, as yet undug.

Erika finally received two food parcels from the women, which she put into her bag. Her sister and brothers came into the living room, still silent and wide-eyed, as though in shock.

Then the moment came: time to say goodbye. Erika was keen to avoid trouble and make sure she got to the rendezvous on time. She slipped on her winter boots and donned the jacket that Grandma Luise had recently knitted for her. Then she put on her heavy winter coat, wrapping the warm scarf and big shawl around her neck. Finally she put on her cap and picked up her bag. Nobody said a word.

Erika hugged the children one last time, patted the cold cheek of her dead grandpa, hugged and kissed her grandma, and then for a few, precious moments found herself in her mother's arms. 'Be brave, my child,' she whispered. Then she let her go, and Erika picked up her suitcase and left the house. No one could see the tears running down her cheeks.

Greta called out after her, 'I put a pack of silk stockings in the case. You'll need them. And don't forget the blade.'

Erika turned and waved one last time with her free hand. 'Goodbye!' she called through her tears. 'God bless you!'

She wondered whether anyone would be wearing silk stockings where she was going.

In front of the Russian commander's house Erika saw some men in boots, heavy coats, fur caps and various other items of winter gear. They looked unfamiliar. She wondered who they were and where they came from. They stood closely together with freezing blue faces. They were carrying various bits of luggage on their backs or in their hands – suitcases, satchels and rucksacks. The men stood there waiting, surrounded by soldiers with guns in their hands. Perhaps they were waiting for the start of their journey to nowhere as well.

No one said a word. Nobody greeted the young lady who came and stood next to the group. They simply looked at her with wondering and pitying eyes, as if to bewail the notion of such a young girl in the clutches of the enemy.

Erika felt a little awkward. She was the only female there. The whole scene felt spooky, with harsh contrasts of bright and dark, and hardly any sound at all. The thick layer of snow muffled what few sounds there were – the squeak of a leather bag, or the faint stomping of feet on the cold ground.

'Come on!' she was ordered harshly. Erika followed the soldier into the house. At least it was warm inside. Just as the day before, she met the elderly officer. But he didn't look so friendly this time. He sat at the table, bent over a sheet of paper that appeared to have a list of names on it.

'Erika Remplin?' he asked abruptly. Erika nodded and saw him put a cross by her name. 'Luggage here!' he ordered, and she put it on the table. One of the soldiers opened her suitcase and checked the contents. He pulled apart all the folded clothes, spreading them on the table. He found nothing to object to. Erika was allowed to put her things back in the suitcase. Next he was more interested in the content of her small bag. He found some apples: when was the last time that he had eaten an apple? They were promptly confiscated. The other men in the room grinned. Erika presumably had to accept it. Protesting didn't feel like an option. At least he'd left her the sandwiches.

'Wait outside for the truck,' the officer finally announced. 'Drive with men to Ciechanow. Then, more deporting.' He signalled the men to leave the room. Erika could only nod again, at the same time feeling an icy shiver run down her spine. To Ciechanow on a truck. She knew it was far away in the east, though she could not recall where she'd heard this.

She picked up her bag and suitcase and went outside. It had started to snow again, but the men were still standing where they had been before. She hoped the truck would come soon. Sitting being driven had to be better than standing in the snow and waiting, feet getting colder by the minute.

Finally, around noon, a monstrous, high-wheeled vehicle arrived. On the open trailer she saw four young soldiers with guns, some more men and, with her back towards the driver's cabin, a girl. Another poor thing, Erika thought. It was going to be a bit cramped when they all got up there, but at least she wasn't going to be alone with all these men.

When the truck had come to a halt the tailgate was opened, the soldiers jumped down from the trailer and took up a guard position. Still hardly anyone spoke. Somebody lifted Erika up and she made a beeline for the girl in the front, sitting herself down next to her. She felt safer there. Hopefully the girl could speak German – the two of them were going to have to stick together on this trip.

Somebody threw Erika's suitcase on top. One at a time the men clambered up, followed by the four soldiers. 'I suppose they need the guards to prevent us from jumping off and trying to escape,' Erika said to herself. Escape! What an idea! What would be the point – where would you go? Anyway, she was done with hiding.

She looked around the truck at the men. Were they Germans or Polish? One of them looked like the sinister man who'd wanted to burn down the village a few days before. So he got caught too. But she wasn't sure it was him. What about Jarek and Jagoda? There was no sign of them. She thought of her family. Would Grandma Luise be able to bury Grandpa Kiel? Would she find somebody who could dig the grave? Would it be done by a Soviet soldier?

So Erika became lost in her thoughts as the smelly truck rattled and roared its way through the deep snow. A pale sun shone through thin clouds, telling them they were heading east. Mercifully the snow had stopped falling.

Before long the truck had crossed the railway line between Torun and Eylau, leaving Gosslershausen far behind. Erika had stayed there just four months. Would she ever come back? Not that that would be her first choice – she'd rather go back to Dortmund and resume her ballet training. Pure fantasy, she told herself – the road now goes east.

It was just as well there were trees on both sides – that way the driver knew where the road was. They were crossing a white desert, interrupted here and there by dark woods. As they passed the trees crows and jackdaws would appear, cawing as they circled the vehicle with its human cargo. Presumably they were after something to eat, but every time they had to fly away disappointed.

At one point they had to slow right down, eventually coming to a complete stop, as they gave way to a seemingly never-ending convoy of Soviet military vehicles. Tanks, troop carriers, transport vehicles large and small – they were all heading back west. It was a noisy and frightening sight. Instinctively Erika took hold of the girl's hand, who gave it eagerly. 'I'm Anna, eighteen, from Rehden,' she whispered.

'I'm Erika. I'm eighteen too.' And that was all they could say, aware that the guards reacted nervously to any movement among the prisoners.

At last the truck began to move again, and they soon reached Strasburg-on-Drewenz. Once more the guards became very fidgety, fearing that someone might try to jump off while they were in the town and disappear behind the next street corner. But they needn't have worried, as it turned out – the little town was crawling with Soviet soldiers. In fact they didn't see a single civilian in any of the narrow streets they took. Where were the Poles who used to live here? Or the Germans? More of her mother's 'wimps and cowards and traitors to the Reich'? But what crime was it to try to save your own life? Erika wondered if the thousands of refugees had arrived at their destination unharmed – somewhere there was no war perhaps. At least they had escaped deportation to the east.

Time would tell who was better off. Who could say just how much further those Soviet tanks would advance into the west? Was there any German defence left at all? Was the 'greatest general of all times' still able to fight back against the enemy?

Erika kept up this curious conversation in her head. She would have loved to talk with Anna about it, but sharp glances and commands from the guards (which sounded like *Ticho!*) told them in no uncertain terms to be quiet. Even so, their hands stayed together. The time may come when they could get to know each other better.

Soon they left the town behind and bumped noisily on their way east. Several times they had to make way for more military convoys. It seemed whole armies were on their way into the German Reich. O, poor Germany, what's going to happen to you?

On one occasion when they were giving way they found themselves stuck in deep snow. But, with a truck-load of men on board, the soldiers knew the answer. Everybody had to get down and push, while the Russians treated themselves to a hearty swig from a bottle. Erika got the impression this 'tea break' was more likely a brief vodka-drinking session.

The two girls were allowed to stay on the truck. They took the opportunity to stand up, stretch their legs and talk a little. Anna told Erika that her father had died a hero in the cauldron of Stalingrad,[2]

---

[2] The brutal Battle of Stalingrad claimed the lives of over 1.5 million people between August 1942 and February 1943.

and that her mother was a nurse stationed in a military hospital near Bromberg. Two older brothers were serving in the war somewhere – she didn't know if they were still alive. Anna herself had been hoping to finish her apprenticeship as a tailor before management training, but now, like Erika, she was starting to give up hope of ever fulfilling her dreams.

Erika quickly told her own story, and then they had to stop talking again. The truck was back on the road and the men were already climbing back up. They hadn't missed the opportunity to talk either, but now they returned to silence as the journey continued. They would reach Ciechanow that night.

This town turned out to be just as full of military personnel, especially the area around the railway station. Under the harsh glare of floodlights, and with deafening noise, devices of war were being unloaded and carried from the tracks to the street. Tanks were thundering, lorry engines roaring, cranes squeaking, and through it all orders were barked out of large loudspeakers. It was an apocalyptic scene and it filled Erika with fear. Fortunately the truck driver was told to keep going, and before long they had left it behind them.

They came to a stop in front of a gloomy, dilapidated shed, and the two girls took each other's hands again. It was much darker here, as the floodlights barely reached this far. 'Everything here is so awful,' Erika whispered to her friend, and gave a shudder.

'You scared?' Anna asked her quietly.

'Yes. But I'm trying to be strong.'

'What will they do with us?' Anna's voice was still low.

'I don't know. The officer back home said we were going to Ciechanow, and then further on. Maybe they'll put us on a train next.'

'But there's no train here,' Anna observed.

'They might bring one once it's been emptied,' Erika mused, and gave Anna's hand a gentle squeeze.

Only the girls had to leave the truck – the men stayed on with three of the guards. There were no helping hands this time, so the girls had to jump down into the muddy snow. Somebody handed them their suitcases, and the truck was gone.

The two young travellers stood closely together, silent, waiting, freezing. A guard stood next to them, gun in hand. Erika wondered if he was freezing too. Actually, she thought, he might not be so badly off – on the journey he had joined his comrades in downing the entire amount of whatever was in those bottles.

After a while, a woman in uniform came along from the direction of the station, accompanied by two men wearing large caps. They were clearly important people. The guard handed over the documents. One of the men unlocked and opened the door to the shed, while a soldier stood on guard. Then the two girls were ordered inside.

They were hit by an unbelievable stench. Hardly able to breathe, they stepped in, aware of a low-level murmuring. As soon as they were right inside, the door behind them was shut and they heard the key being turned.

'Welcome to the monkey-cage . . . or the pigsty!' croaked a woman's voice out of a corner. It took the girls a few moments to get used to the darkness in the shed. Practically no light came through the small and dirty windows. Soon they could see people strewn all over the ground, dozing or sleeping, some simply sitting, staring ahead. Erika wondered where they'd all come from, and what they'd been through.

The cracked voice came again out of the darkness. 'Did they catch you as well, you poor creatures? Not quick enough, eh?' They could just about make out the outlined form of the woman. She'd got up and was now approaching them through the space in the middle of the room. 'Oh, they're going to want a taste of you two! The Russians love fresh flesh. Best line up ready!' The woman laughed bitterly at her own remark, then shook the hands of the young newcomers and, as if she were their commanding officer, showed them to a place at the back of the room.

Neither Erika nor Anna felt able to speak. The woman's words had left them in shock. What on earth was coming to them? They sat with their backs to the wall, silent and afraid, holding each other's hands.

'Don't take it too seriously, you two; Heide's a bit course.' A woman next to them spoke reassuringly out of the gloom.

'Is there a toilet here?' Erika asked. 'I've not been able to . . .'

'Me neither,' Anna added.

'Sure – there's a big bucket next to the door. That's all we've got, I'm afraid,' the woman said. But at this Heide felt the need to pass a comment. 'Don't be embarrassed,' she cawed. 'Just imagine there are Russians inside it – they deserve everything you can aim at them!' Once more she laughed at her own remark, but this time she was scolded from another corner. 'Watch your tongue, Heide. You could get us all into trouble.'

Heide mumbled something indignantly, but that was the last they heard from her for the rest of the night. Gradually the general murmuring gave way to an oppressive silence, which made it even harder for Erika and Anna to go to the toilet, complete with the inevitable sound effects. But before very much longer they had no choice, and reluctantly, under the welcome cover of darkness, they did what they had to do, suffering the stench. There was no paper.

Afterwards the two girls made their beds on the ground. Erika's coat served as a mattress, while Anna's was big enough to become their blanket. 'I hope they leave us alone,' Anna whispered. 'I'm so scared they might . . .'

'I know. I'm worried about them "wanting a taste" too, but I'll pray that it won't happen. God can help.'

'You believe in God – and you a BDM girl!'

'I was a BDM girl,' Erika insisted. 'And I don't know if I believe in God. But I do pray to him. He can help.'

'Then pray for me as well. I can't. And sleep well, Erika.'

'You too, Anna. We'll know by tomorrow whether God has helped or not.'

Things were quietening down outside. The men who had been loading were apparently taking a nocturnal break. The room was now very quiet – just the sound of regular breathing and the occasional sigh or cough.

Suddenly Erika was woken by the creaking sound of the door. She had no idea what time it was. Two men entered with flashlights. They walked around, shining the torches over the sleeping women, clearly looking for 'fresh flesh'.

'God, help us now!' Erika prayed in a silent scream. She moved even closer to Anna who was sleeping deeply, totally unaware of what was going on, despite the growing unrest. Erika turned her own face away.

After a few moments the two men left the shed again, dragging two struggling women after them.

'Thank God!' was all that went through Erika's mind. They were spared, this time at least. God had answered her prayer. But those poor women . . .

A little later Erika fell asleep. The two girls slept until they were woken up by a light in the room and the order to get up and get ready. It would have helped if the lamp had been a little brighter. But what right did prisoners have to light?

During the minutes that followed the women got up from the hard ground and, one after the other, went to the toilet. It was Heide who used her own coat to shield them a little, for which all of them were extremely grateful, even if the light was very dim. Perhaps there was more to Heide than they'd thought.

Both the night's victims had also returned, though Erika didn't know quite when. It was obvious what they'd been through.

There were about forty women in all, the oldest about forty-five. They arranged their clothes, packed their bags and waited for orders. Soon they were told to line up in pairs in front of the shed. A welcoming committee was already standing in the cold morning, keeping an eye on a large group of other women who had also lined up ready. They must have spent the night some-where else.

It was snowing again, but at least the air was fresh. After the stench in the shed it was a relief to breathe deeply out here. Some of the women exchanged a few words, but no one talked much. Most of them seemed to be thinking about what was going to happen on the second stage of their deportation.

They didn't have to wait long for an answer. Another troop of soldiers soon turned up, this time led by a woman. She apparently knew one German phrase, no doubt learned for this mission: 'Come with me!' she barked, and led them away.

The soldiers marched the group through the snow to where all that noise and busyness was going on. A new freight train had clearly arrived, and currently more engines of war and troops were being unloaded. Then Erika and Anna saw an empty train with an assortment of wagons, some flat and open and some with roofs on. There was only one wagon designed to carry passengers.

'They're going to transport us on this!' Anna exclaimed as they walked, the incredulity rising in her voice.

'Weapons one way, victims the other,' Erika replied.

'But those are cattle wagons . . . we're not animals!' Anna protested.

'Don't worry, they'll soon be treating us like animals,' interrupted a woman walking in front of them. 'And you can bet that passenger truck's not got our names on it!'

'Just so long as they don't put us in the open wagons,' said Erika. 'That would be awful.'

Heide decided it was time to join the conversation. 'True, we'd soon catch our deaths out in this cold and wet . . . but maybe that's what they want. Why feed us and keep us warm? They don't give a toss about who dies when, or where they do it.'

Anna thought differently. 'I reckon they're sending us to a labour camp to let us work ourselves to death. After all, that's what the Germans did with Russian prisoners who were brought to the Reich. Why are we going to be any better off?'

'Tit for tat,' Erika mumbled; 'an eye for an eye and a tooth for a tooth . . . isn't that what they say? Oh, but I hope they show us some mercy.'

'We'll soon find out,' was Heide's last word on the matter, for now the group were arriving at the train, and the commander stopped in front of an enclosed goods wagon. Its large sliding door stood wide open. The women peered inside. There was nothing. Absolutely nothing – nothing to sit on, nothing to lie on. 'Worse than animals,' thought Erika. 'They'd at least spread out some straw for them.'

There were no windows, only some slits in the wall, though these were too high for a short person like Erika to reach. There was going to be precious little light and air. Erika wondered if there was a bucket, at least, that they could use as a toilet. She could forget being able to wash her hands – or any other part of her body. The mere thought was enough to make her feel sick. This was going to be a tough and dirty ride, and, with no heater and the open slits, freezing cold. But there was one luxury at least: the wagon had a roof. This time they would be dry.

'Get in!' It seemed the female officer knew two German phrases, and she pointed to the open door. But how were they supposed to climb up without a ladder? These Russian trains were much higher than those back in Germany. The larger gauge of the tracks presumably determined that.

'Get in! *Dawai!*' the woman repeated more harshly. The women had no choice but to beat the snow off their clothes and help each other into the wagon. Those on the ground helped to heave others up, who once inside hauled the rest in. It was strenuous work, coloured by a good deal of complaining and cursing. The Russian officer took no notice, and simply told them to get a move on. Meanwhile the guards were far too entertained by the whole process to actually offer any kind of help.

Happily Erika and Anna were among the first who were helped into the wagon. Erika was so light it took no real effort to get her inside. And no one was expecting her or Anna to pull anyone else in – the other women were bigger and stronger. So the two girls took the opportunity to choose a place. They went for one of the corners, sitting on the dirty floor with their legs drawn up and their suitcases behind their backs. They were ready to defend this place if any of the others challenged them. At last they began to feel a bit safer – almost comfortable. Anything was better than having to sit in the middle of the wagon, or close to the door.

As soon as all the women were inside, the door was closed from the outside and securely locked. Perhaps the Russians were afraid the women would revolt because of their conditions, thought Erika. As if.

Gradually, as their eyes became accustomed to the light, so the women's fear began to diminish, and they started to talk. Not that they liked what their eyes now told them. Soon they were complaining, cursing and swearing at the Russian 'rats and pigs', and fights inevitably broke out over who was going to sit where. The cramped conditions meant a good deal of shoving and pushing. And, with nearly fifty women trying to find a suitable spot in the crowded darkness, it soon became incredibly noisy. Few of them were pleased with what they found, and even fewer could lie down at all, or stretch their limbs. There were bodies and suitcases everywhere.

Clearly they were going to have to set up some rules. One of them had to take a lead if they were going to avoid a real fight, and it was Heide who shouted them down. At last there was some quiet.

'This isn't going to work,' she said. 'We've got to get on with each other. Who knows how long we're going to be travelling like this? There's no use in making life even harder by fighting. One of us has to be in charge. We need to get ourselves organised.'

There was a murmur of general agreement. Then someone piped up: 'Why don't you take over – you're used to it. You were leader of the Women's Guild.' Again there was general consent.

'All right, if you really think so. I'll give it a go.' And so the new leader got straight to sorting things out. She showed the women where to sit, and how, so that there was enough room in case somebody really had to lie down. And they had to reserve some space for something like a toilet, as 'those stupid barbarians' had not even provided them with a bucket. And if they needed something like a place where food was going to be handed out then that clearly shouldn't be right next to the toilet.

After a while, some real order came to the wagon. Meanwhile the train had not gone anywhere yet. Some of the women had watches and checked the time. It was already late in the afternoon, and in the wagon at least it was almost completely dark. Suddenly the door was opened again and a woman in civilian clothes with a Red Cross badge over her arm – accompanied by the inevitable soldiers – shoved in a cardboard box with bread and another with aluminium cups. Then one of the soldiers heaved in a container with some sort of liquid in it, before closing the door again. Clearly their tormentors didn't intend them to starve.

Heide distributed the bread and the drinks. There were not enough cups for everyone. Erika and Anna happily shared. The bread wasn't much, but it was still better than nothing. Heide – whom by now they were calling 'Chief' – decided that the two cardboard boxes were to be used as covers for the 'toilet'.

By the time it was pitch black outside the women began to talk a little about themselves. If nothing else it would help pass the time, and getting to know each other had to ease the awful situation a little. They kept it up for ages, even after the train had left Ciechanow in the middle of the night, and on again during the days that followed. Where they were going nobody knew.

Every now and then the train would stop for quite a while. If it was daytime one of the women would look through the slits, but all she could see was unknown, snow-covered land or endless forest. They seldom stopped at a station, and the names usually meant nothing to them – except that a young teacher, who was called Else, was able to help out a couple of times. She told them that Biatystok was in East Prussia, Baranowicze and Minsk in White Russia. But then she couldn't explain to them why the train stopped in Kiev a couple of days later, since that was in the south, in Ukraine. The route was a complete mystery.

Maybe this was why, as the days drew on, they began to feel quite desperate. They did get food once a day, though the hunks of bread and dried meat were nowhere near enough to fill their stomachs. And the small rations of weak tea were no better. Meanwhile the temperature was falling steadily. The growing cold and the lack of hygiene inevitably gave rise to various forms of sickness, such as coughs, colds, gastric flu and fever, and even the doctor among them went down with something.

The first death came after a week. The poor woman had coughed herself to death. At one of their routine stops for food and air – which were always made miles from anywhere so no one tried to escape – the body was simply tossed out, along with the excrement, so much food for the wolves. They kept the clothes in the wagon 'in memory', and the women used them as a mattress and blankets.

More deaths followed; more bodies thrown into the snow. By now all traces of laughter were gone, and no one was singing. A general lethargy came over everyone.

Through all this horror Erika was surprised to find she remained in fairly good spirits, and her health held up too. Both she and Anna seemed to have accepted their fate. They weren't about to burst into song, but nor did they grumble, or curse, or kick up a fuss like the other women. Instead they encouraged each other and tried to stay positive. Somehow they were going to endure. Erika's thoughts came back to the God she didn't know very well.

She talked it over with Anna, but it turned out she had even less knowledge about real Christian faith. She'd been born Catholic, but had grown up in a totally National Socialist home where Christian belief had never been a factor. From what Aunt Erna had said, Erika realised that her friend was a deist. She had some vague notion of a God 'up there' who had probably started the whole thing off but had absolutely no involvement with what they were going through now on this miserable journey – nor with those who were dying.

If only it wasn't so cold! With only forty of them left the combined body heat was no longer enough to bring the temperature above freezing, and the walls started to ice up. The cold began to creep under the women's clothes and into their flesh. Even the extra clothes from those who had died didn't help. So now hypothermia and frostbite struck several of the women, and though Heide had them all on a strict regime of exercises these poor folk could not take part. Erika and Anna tried to prevent frostbite by taking off their boots and socks twice a day and rubbing each other's feet, as well as doing their exercises in what little room they had. Erika's ballet training was proving a lifesaver.

But how they longed for a real meal, for light and warmth, for enough room to stretch out, for space to move freely, for fresh air, for water to wash in . . . and for something to *do*, to fill the day with a sense of purpose, even if it was in captivity. When would this nightmare end?

CHAPTER 5

Life at Camp

At last the journey was over. According to the marks one of the women had scratched into the walls, they had been travelling for fourteen days, and it must have been February when the train finally came to a prolonged halt. This time they heard dull sounds coming from outside. They were mixed up with the hissing and wheezing of the locomotive, so the women weren't sure just what they were, but they came from one side of the train at a time.

The women grew uneasy. Everyone wanted to know what was going on. One of the women was lifted up to peer outside, and she told them what she saw. 'There's a tall wire fence, and beyond that I can see a street leading up through a forest. The sun's so bright. There are some cars and trucks, and there's a group of people walking – I can't see their faces as they've got thick hoods on. No buildings this side.'

As in fact most of the sounds were coming from the other side of the train, they switched over to take a look in that direction. Here, beyond some more railway tracks, the woman could see several low, barrack-like buildings. There was a big house and a storage building where it looked like wood was being milled, as there were huge piles of tree trunks. Behind the storage building the woman made out several large factories. Smoke was rising through the roofs.

'I think we've reached our destination.' The woman climbed back down. 'There's bright sunshine outside,' she repeated.

'Lovely . . . we'll go for a stroll then, shall we?' said one of the others with a forced laugh.

'They'll take us for a walk soon enough,' said another. 'Unfortunately, I won't be able to come along,' she added with a sigh. 'My legs just won't do it.'

Now all the women tried to stand. Several found the frostbite made it impossible.

'Okay Anna, let's get ready for freedom!' said Erika as she patted her friend on the shoulder.

'I dunno,' she replied. 'I'm scared.'

'What are you scared of, Anna?'

'The work we might have to do here. I'm too weak.'

'If the Russians want us to work they'll give us food. It would be pointless otherwise.' Erika sounded confident.

'And I'm scared of the men here,' Anna persisted. 'What if they like their "fresh flesh" as well?'

'Then we'll pray just as we did in Ciechanow.'

'Do you really think it would protect us again?'

'I hope so. But we'll just have to face things as they come. Anyway,' she changed tack, 'I'd like to take a look out there now.'

'Come here, Little Flea, I'll lift you,' Heide offered. This was the new name for the lightest girl in the company. 'What do you see?'

'I can see people coming in our direction. They'll probably take us with them. There are at least five of them, and one is a woman. She looks like a giant.'

'Everyone looks like a giant to you!' said one of the women behind her.

'Are they armed?' Heide wanted to know.

'The men are carrying guns, but not the woman. She's got a . . . a folder in her hand, or something like that.' Erika climbed back down. 'It can't be long now till we're out in the fresh air.'

'I hope they have a decent feeding trough and a warm bath lined up,' one of the women said.

'And a nice hot cup of tea,' said another.

'I could use a hot toddy,' added a third.

'That wouldn't do you any good,' the doctor put in. 'With our frostbite and stomach upsets, what we need most of all right now is a proper doctor.'

'You mean a vet, for the poor pigs!' observed Anna. 'And they've probably not even got one of those!'

'You always look on the dark side,' Erika objected. 'That just makes life worse than it already is.'

'Our Little Flea is right,' Heide chimed in. 'We should wait and see what comes. And then – we'll need to stick together, and be there for one another, as much as we can.'

'I hope they let us stay together, now we've got to know each other,' said one of the others.

'As I say, we'll see,' said 'Chief' Heide. 'Here comes the reception committee.'

Already they could hear voices outside, getting nearer all the time. Then the bolt of the wagon door was undone and the door was slid open. The light of the low noon sun flooded the interior, and with that a wave of cold but fresh air. For a moment the women could neither see nor breathe.

Even so, this moment seemed so wonderful to Erika that for a few seconds she forgot where she was. The smooth, rich voice of the Russian woman brought her back to reality. It was almost soothing – Erika hoped she'd have a personality to match. She certainly seemed to be in command right now.

'Major Natali,' she introduced herself as she looked up at them all. 'Please to get out. Has come end of your journey.' Erika noted the 'please'.

'Please to get out and make line,' the woman repeated.

One after the other, as they were able, the women jumped down into the snow. Down on the ground they noticed that several other wagons, apparently also filled with women, had joined their own. The one carrying the men was nowhere to be seen.

'What about others?' the major asked.

Heide was still on the wagon: 'They can't jump – their feet are frostbitten. They can't even stand, never mind jump.'

The woman seemed to understand, but simply commanded, 'Then help down!'

'And how are they supposed to stand and walk?' Heide implored with mounting anger.

'Must hold them. Get out now! *Dawai, dawai!*' Her voice had definitely lost its smooth tone. And with that she turned to the next wagon, where the door had already been opened, and repeated her routine. The soldiers stood by, keeping guard – as if anyone had either the courage or the strength to cause trouble.

At last all the women stood or sat in the snow next to their empty wagons, and the second part of the reception got under way. The major read the passenger list out loud to each group. She ticked the names of those who were there and crossed out those who were absent on account of death in transit. She told every woman which barracks they were assigned to.

'*Barak* number one!' she barked; '*barak* number two!' So she went on, and on, and the cold began to slide its icy fingers under the women's clothes once more, taking no notice of the pale wintry sun which was doing its best to welcome the women to their new abode.

After about an hour they were done. The major called, 'Follow! *Dawai!*' and the soldiers surrounded them, keeping their distance. Exhausted, the women followed the leader who had to keep stopping to wait for the trail of miserable figures to catch up. Finally she stopped between some long, low buildings, each about six metres wide, where she turned round and made the women line up again.

'Wait here!' she demanded. Then she pointed at some women who seemed a bit stronger than the rest, gave them a large broom each and ordered them to clean the barracks. They were the lucky ones – the remaining 120 women had to stand and wait in the freezing cold.

Eventually the cleaners finished, and as they emerged their faces told the others in no uncertain terms just how comfortable their new quarters were not going to be.

The major too had not moved during this time, but now she pointed at the barracks around them and shouted, '*Barak* one. *Barak* two. *Barak* three. *Tualet* back there. Now move!'

The women assembled together according to barracks number, and shuffled off, stopping on the way at the latrine. This was very basic, with no proper roof to shield them from the outdoors. Even so, it was better than the facilities of the last two weeks.

Happily, Erika and Anna had been assigned to the same barracks. They looked for a place to sleep – a place to live – somewhere not too near the door, for fear of the dreaded nocturnal visits they knew might occur. The girls skipped the toilet so they could claim a place in the back of the room before anyone else could take it. It was nothing more than a wooden floor, bare and cold, no better than the wagon. No wooden pallets even, or hay matresses. 'Surely,' thought Erika, 'we don't treat Russian foreign workers in Germany this primitively. We really are worse off than animals!'

The barracks' entire furniture consisted of a large table made from rough timber, set in the middle of the room with some chairs round it. There was just one oil lamp for extra light – not that much light shone through the tiny windows anyway. There was no fire or any other way of heating the room. Time to freeze again. But there was one good thing: all forty of the women had room to stretch themselves out!

About an hour later a command erupted from the doorway: 'All stand at bed place!' Some of the women were able to comply; some plainly were not, and they remained lying down on their coats or their blankets, or draped over a chair. Natali – the major they had already met – walked past the rows of women, accompanied by two other women in uniform. At each place they bent down and ransacked their victim's bag, always finding something they objected to . . . something they could use. An item of underwear here, an article of clothing there. The confiscated items disappeared into a big bag. Any protest – noisy or quiet – was answered with a sharp '*Ticho!*' The two armed soldiers at the door simply grinned.

That's one way of getting your stuff, Erika thought, as she braced herself for the violation of her own baggage. But all they took was a piece of soap and a brush. Not that she could think any of them would want her clothes anyway – she was a size 8! And what use was soap when she had nowhere to wash? And where was the mirror while she was supposedly brushing her hair? Aunt Erna flashed into Erika's thoughts: 'Have as though you do not have.' It was starting to make sense now.

They had taken several items of clothing from Anna, who was size 14. 'You're lucky to be a flea, Erika,' Anna said with a touch of envy. But this flea had courage, and decided to speak up and ask the officer when they would be given something to eat and drink. '*Potom*, later,' was the gruff response. 'Little person can wait.'

Erika murmured something suitably disrespectful under her breath, earning a sharp '*Ticho!*'

In the evening the major and her two henchwomen returned, this time without the soldiers. They brought a large basket of bread with them, a huge saucepan of hot porridge, and another large container with hot tea, which they set down on the table. At last . . . after two weeks of hard bread and cold tea, something warm to eat and drink! Warm *káscha* and hot *tschaj*. It was bliss.

All at once forty German women made a dash for the food, hunger and thirst driving them on. 'Chief' Heide stepped in quickly, calling for order. 'There's enough here for everyone! Anyway, you're hardly going to eat porridge out of your hands now, are you!'

Right on cue a delivery boy came in, suitably equipped with a large number of bowls and spoons. They looked cheap, Erika thought, but brand new. The boy was greeted with applause and every resident of this fine hotel was given a set for herself. Now they were ready for the bread and porridge! Those who had no cup could drink the tea out of the bowl when the porridge was gone. Such luxury.

'Slowly!' Major Natali ordered, while promising to supply them with more cups. Then she asked: 'Who's in charge in barracks?'

'Heide, you do it.' There was no hesitation from the women from Heide's wagon, and none of the women from the other wagons objected either. Heide agreed, and introduced herself to the major as their duly elected chief.

Natali eyed the woman up and down, and clearly considered her qualified. 'You responsible for *distschhiplina*. All must be in order, quiet and clean. Understand?'

'I understand!' Heide replied. Then she asked for a doctor for the women with frostbite and other problems.

'No *doktorscha*, maybe later,' was the answer.

'Please, tomorrow then – we need a doctor badly,' she repeated, but got straight to organising the food distribution.

Then, with what was presumably a curt 'goodnight', the Russians left the women to their first warm meal in two weeks – and to a night where they were all finally able to stretch out. Even so, they needed to stay fairly close so as not to lose what precious warmth they had in the icy room.

No one came the next day. Nobody knew where they were, or what was going to happen to them. They made the most of the time by resting, and hoped that their questions would be answered the next day.

At eight o'clock the next morning, Major Natali returned with her adjutants and a middle-aged officer of higher rank. They greeted the women with a loud and friendly phrase that clearly meant 'good morning' and told them to get up from their sleeping places. They came armed with a few folders and a heap of papers, but they also brought bread and tea for breakfast. While Heide was in charge of handing out the breakfast, the Russian women and the officer occupied the table. They summoned the women one at a time to come to the table to answer questions. Everybody else had to stay quiet.

The questioning took ages. Following each interview the four people at the table conferred and made a decision. They seemed to be as concerned with outward appearance as with apparent state of health.

Erika's turn came in the afternoon. They asked her about her life, her family, and her opinion of Adolf Hitler and National Socialism. As in every other case the officer asked the questions and Major Natali translated back and forth, though nobody was there to check whether she translated correctly. When they learned that little Erika wanted to be a dancer, they smiled – or was it a smirk? Erika wasn't sure whether it was friendly or not. No doubt time would tell.

The questioning finally came to an end in the early evening. Heide then had to choose some of the women to fetch the food from now on, and others had to look after cleaning the place. Her request for a doctor was deferred again.

Anna was one of those put in charge of getting the food, much to Erika's disappointent; she would have jumped at the chance to get outside at least once a day, to see somewhere different and maybe meet other people. But they didn't want the camp flea to carry the heavy kettles and pots, or even to swing a broom, it seemed. Erika was to take care of the weak and the sick, to help them eat and get them going. So that's what she did. She even sang 'Heidschi Bumbeidschi' to them. Whatever it took.

But, when the Russians had left them again that night, they still had no idea what was going to happen to them.

That night they ate bread and something like cabbage soup, though they'd have needed a magnifying glass to spot the cabbage. This was to become their main dish from now on.

Two days later it was Saturday, and the women were told to line up in front of the barracks to go to the baths. They were to take new clothes and towels with them. At last . . . an opportunity to wash! They lined up in great excitement, the weak ones held up by the others – apart from the really sick who, to Erika's horror, had to remain behind and stay dirty.

The 'bath' turned out to be the dirty, greasy washroom of the factory that was situated outside the perimeter, on the other side of a gate guarded by several uniformed men. It was quite a trek, and when they got there they found no bathtub, just a few buckets lined up along the walls. But at least they could have a proper wash, pouring water over themselves and washing their hair. After a moment's hesitation even the women who were embarrassed were standing naked in front of the tubs.

Erika sensed that the other women saw her as little more than a doll, and she shot a look of envy at those who had a bit more to show than she did. But then the water soon made her forget all that. It wasn't what you'd call warm, but it wasn't freezing either. Nobody seemed to care any more that there was no heating. They helped the ones who couldn't wash themselves due to their rheumatic or frostbitten limbs, and they hoped this wasn't going to be a one-off event.

An hour later the women had finished washing and were all dressed again. It felt like being newborn, even if they were wearing their old clothes. And they weren't freezing any more. They had been ordered to leave their dirty underwear in a barrel for washing. Some were only too pleased, but others suspected they would never see their things again. They were right.

When they got back to the barracks the happy mood soon changed again. They had to line up in the centre of the room, no matter what state of health they were in. Major Natali read out a list of places for everyone to work, including the sick. Many faces turned pale when they learned that they were to work in the woods the next day, and that they had to clean up an evacuated military hospital before that.

Heide saw red. 'How are women with frostbite supposed to work at all, never mind in the woods where it's below freezing? We need a doctor present!' There were murmurs of agreement.

But it was no use arguing. 'No *doktorscha!*' came the sharp response. Her one concession: 'Those who really cannot walk, remain lying down. Rest of you, seven o'clock ready for work.'

'But tomorrow's Sunday,' somebody dared to object.

'What is Sunday?' was the angry reply. 'For you, all days are work.'

'Do we get work clothes?' Heide put in.

'Trousers, jacket, boots, gloves,' the Russian woman replied, and the women all sighed with relief. 'More question?' she asked them sharply.

'Will you give us food?' Heide begged, but all she got in response was, 'Will not starve.' Then the commander told them to step aside and she left the hut. Some of the women wondered what work they would be doing.

But before that, there was a night to get through . . .

It was late. Suddenly loud and rough voices could be heard, first outside the barracks and then much closer. Several men came in with lamps in their hands. They stopped at the doorway.

'They're looking for their fresh flesh,' thought Erika, and softly she nudged Anna. Oh God, how would this turn out? Would they pick her?

'You'll have to pray, Little Flea,' Anna whispered in her friend's ear. 'You said in Ciechanow that praying works.'

Erika had to admit to herself that she hadn't prayed since then, at least not consciously. But now was the time to start again. 'God, please help us once more. We're still so young. Please, don't let them . . . please, God, help us!' She clasped her hands together as she whispered her prayer.

One of the men walked through the room and counted in Polish, picking out women as he went. It was no use pleading, or complaining, or cursing either. Each woman had to comply, knowing only too well what was coming.

'God, let him not pick us!' Erika prayed. The man stopped at three – Anna would have been number four. 'Thank you, God,' she said with a sigh of relief. They had been spared, at least on this occasion.

The nightly visits continued on and off. Each time they counted – one time it might be to four, the next to seven, depending on the number of men looking to satisfy their 'hunger'. Yet each time Erika was spared. Erika was amazed, and the God Aunt Erna had introduced her to slowly became more and more real to her. If only she knew more about him! But none of the other women believed in God, so her questions went unanswered. She had to make do with 'the Lord is with me; he is my helper' and simply determined to learn more about him once she was home again – whenever that might be.

But Anna found no such mercy. Again and again she was among those used by the men. Railing against her fate, she told Erika she wanted to hear nothing more about her trust in God or her pointless prayers. She rebuffed Erika's attempts to console her, and the relationship soon cooled. Anna became distant as she hardened herself more and more. Even so Erika tried to remain buoyant in the midst of it all.

Meanwhile the work they had to do was getting harder and harder, taking all their strength. It had been simple enough to clean the military hospital, but working in the woods quickly left many of them exhausted. Each morning, at dawn, they travelled by open truck into the woods. The hour-long journey took them through the ruined town of Charkow. So now they knew exactly where they were; it seemed that just about all the supposedly Russian people here were actually Ukrainians.

They had to work seven days a week in all weathers – snow, rain, dense fog, bright sun. Sometimes the ground was frozen hard as stone; sometimes it turned into a knee-deep swamp. But the prisoners had targets to meet – if they missed them, they were given less food and generally harassed. Days off were rare.

Their Ukrainian tormentors thought nothing of health problems or mental anguish. Those who had no strength any more were considered useless, and certainly not worthy of special treatment in terms of nutrition or medicine. With a steady supply of new inmates arriving to take their place, it was simpler to just leave them to die.

And that is what a great number of the women did. Over the months, as they fell victim to exhaustion, weakness and misery, their names were simply crossed out at the weekly roll-calls. And that was that. Were any relatives back home notified, or maybe sent some item of personal belongings? Hardly – all the ones deemed valuable had already been taken away from them. The rest of their belongings were inherited by the remaining prisoners. After a while nobody worried about wearing clothes that had come off a corpse.

Eventually some 300 women remained in the camp.

Spring finally came, but it brought few changes to their living or working conditions. The work in the forest was done, so now they moved to the fields that belonged to several farming collectives in the region around Charkow. Some of these were so large you couldn't see where they ended. The work consisted of planting vegetables and then cultivating and watering them – cabbage, potatoes, beet and tomatoes. Erika found this work easier, even though the tools they were given didn't help very much.

Once again their targets were high. From eight in the morning till eight at night they had to work the land. Thousands of new vegetable plants had to be planted and watered in – potatoes by the hundredweight, thousands of beets, and hundreds of tomato seedlings, all needing to be planted and hoed. The job was even harder when the sun burned down on them and their water rations remained as low as ever. Those who were doing the watering soon gave in to the temptation to drink some of the water for the plants, dirt and all.

As for food, there was none – not in the day. In the mornings they ate a few slices of *chljeb s-warjénim*, bread with marmalade, which on rare occasions was upgraded to *chljeb s-mjássam*, bread with meat. The portions were tiny. The drink was always *tschaj*, a thin liquid supposed to be tea. If anyone got caught taking a slice of bread and putting it under her jacket, there was no breakfast the next day.

In the evenings it was cabbage soup and bread. Every day.

Hunger was their constant companion, but Erika was one of several who came up with a solution – the young, fresh cabbage plants turned out to be edible. And the more they ate, the fewer they had to plant, which was a bonus. They also ate raw potatoes. The stomach aches and diarrhoea that followed became normal. And out on the fields the only thing that bothered them was the missing paper . . .

Wednesday the 9th May 1945 turned out to be different. It became a day of special favours, which nonplussed everybody – some were bordering on happiness. Major Natali made an announcement in her simple German, concocted from her usual blend of satisfied pride and sarcasm. This was a historical day, it seemed. The women pricked up their ears. Erika wondered what was coming; what could be so exciting this early in the morning?

What she heard she could scarcely believe. The first thing the major told them was that, since the 30th April, 'the greatest general of all time', he who had caused such terrible and widespread misery among the Soviets, was no more. This inhumane monster had avoided liability by committing suicide, leaving his army and his people to their fate. The brave Soviet armies had fought back victoriously. Berlin, the capital, had fallen. The glorious Soviet Army had forced the German Empire into surrender – a surrender that had been announced the previous day, the 8th May. The war was finally over. Germany was crushed and would not rise again any time soon.

All this was cause for celebration for the people of the victorious Soviet Union. And as a special favour for the vanquished, and in honour of the occasion, the women did not have to work that day. Hip hip hooray.

Naturally the women's applause was muted – not that it meant a lot to most of them. They had long since broken with the Reich and its Führer. Only a few had remained loyal to the victory slogans that had now sunk below defeat and despair. Yet even these welcomed the day off.

The celebrations continued with an extra meal at noon. It was *saljánka*, a soup with added vegetables and meat. The women went for a walk in the spring sun that flooded the camp in its

warm, bright light. If only their future were as warm and bright!
But Major Natali had given no hint of change. The Soviets would
presumably now need time to plan for the future.

Erika made the most of the day: the bright sunshine, the
warmth of spring, the flowers under the trees where the first
patches of green were visible, the birdsong. For one day she could
enjoy this all freely and openly. But the space gave Erika time to
think of other things too. She had been away from home for three
months now, though it had seemed an age. She'd not been able to
write, nor had she heard a thing. In fact, now she thought about
it, she had never seen anyone receiving or writing a letter.

Erika wondered whether they really had any reason to hope for
a return home any time soon. Might the Russians and the
Ukrainians not want to extend their revenge a bit longer? Perhaps
she should pray. God had protected her from the men's night-time
visits; maybe he could also help her get home soon.

She thought of her mother. Her convictions – her illusions –
must finally have been shattered. Was she free? Or had she been
deported somewhere as well? Perhaps she too was 'fresh flesh' . . .?
And what about her father? She wondered if he was still even
alive. And what about the rest of her family – did they finally get
to bury Grandpa Kiel?

She guessed that Anna was having similar thoughts. Even on
this special day they exchanged no more than a few words before
parting again. It seemed that Erika's answers to prayer had
erected a barrier between them. Anna was often selected at night
– proof to Anna that Erika's prayers were selfish, or simply didn't
work at all.

The evening roll-call and distribution of *káscha* and *chljeb*
brought Erika back to reality. She shrugged. She couldn't work it

out, but she was determined not to lose her hope for a safe return. She refused to become like those women who had given up hope for a better future.

The reality of it all hit home with brutal force when, later that night, the men paid another visit, clearly drunk from the day's celebrations. Once again Erika was spared, and Anna was not. She went without a word.

The next morning the Ukrainian guards and the soldiers were in an ill temper. Clearly they had drunk more than usual – though this meant they were very lax in their guard duties. They lay on the ground and slept it all off, leaving the women free to talk, stretch their aching limbs, and drink the water meant for the plants.

So came one more day of freedom. But it was not to last.

CHAPTER 6

Moving On

Erika struggled through camp life near war-torn Charkow, enduring the work in both forest and field. But she mourned for several days when Anna did not return from a night-time visit and was simply crossed off the list at the weekly roll-call. She hated to think about what might have happened.

Lena was now the new 'chief', having taken over Heide's role as spokeswoman in 'number one barracks'. She told the young Erika nothing about what had happened to Anna, but said that she would be benefiting from Anna's disappearance by 'inheriting' her belongings.

The warm clothes were welcome enough, even if they were too big. Sleeves could always be rolled up – and it wasn't as if any of the women at camp would have won a fashion prize – or an award for beauty for that matter. Most of them had had their heads shaved because of the lice, and they could only wash once every few weeks. They had skin problems. And, of course, no change of clothes. Nor any real chance to wash them. They couldn't smell the body odour any more. If there was something they chose not to wear, then sooner or later it was confiscated – their Ukrainian minders needed clothes and underwear too. If there was a hole in something, you had to live with it. The sewing needles some of the women still had on arrival at the camp had long since fallen foul of the many inspections.

Major Natali had been a fairly friendly soul who had mostly refrained from harassing them. However, a few days after the celebration of the end of the war and the German surrender, another woman had taken her place. Maybe the 'holiday' had been Natali's doom?

She was succeeded by Svetlana, a very pretty woman of about thirty, with a sharp tongue and a heart full of vengeance, a fact she let them know again and again in almost perfect German. She had been liberated when the Soviets had invaded the defeated German Reich, and had returned to her home in the Ukraine. Here she had taken on the job in the women's camp near Charkow. One of her first official acts had been to give Heide's job to Lena. Erika tried to keep her distance because Lena seemed to prefer to say what the camp leadership wanted to hear – and whatever was in her own interest.

Erika had to fight her way through the next winter, working in the forest again in anything down to 40 degrees below zero. Sometimes they worked at the nearby factory, where they had to shovel coal from carts and transport them into bunkers. It was dirty work, and hard. Erika's shovel was almost bigger than her and really heavy. Her lungs were soon full of coal dust. Even so, one advantage here was the opportunity to wash more often – not every day but at least every time they had to unload the wagons.

Then there was the sawdust to load in the nearby sawmill, which was quite easy work. The sawdust was not as heavy as coal, and while it was dusty at least it wasn't black. And they only had to work for as long as the regular workers, which meant ten hours and not one minute more. The Ukrainians were very strict about this – not a problem for Erika and her fellow workers.

And so the winter passed, and Erika got on well enough. But come the end a big surprise was waiting, as a hundred of them were summoned together for transportation. Given that the war had been over for more than a year, they thought they must be heading home . . . Those whose names were read out became excited, and Erika was ecstatic when her name was called. At last they were going home! Thank God!

But tears were soon to follow, and anger, as Svetlana informed them they were going to Russia, to a region south of Moscow called Tula, where workers were needed in the state-run collective farms. The Russian agricultural system needed building up again after the war – a war that had been brought upon the country by Germans. 'So . . . no reason to make a fuss,' sneered the officer with a grin as she explained what was happening, clearly loving every minute of it.

Erika would have loved to tell Svetlana what she thought of her, but she had learnt to hold her peace. So she just wiped the tears from her face with the sleeve of her jacket, and left the other women to yell and curse over the fact that the officer had decided to string them along before finally telling them they weren't going home.

But who was to say this wasn't actually one more step towards home? So Erika told herself to swallow her anger and disappointment, and make the best of it. 'God's been with you here and he's helped you – and he'll be with you in Tula too.' She didn't know where this way of thinking came from, but she welcomed it like a new friend.

Like all the other women whose names were on the transportation list, Erika packed her belongings into her suitcase and bag and prepared to leave the next morning. Unfortunately, it was still too early for *chljeb* and *tschaj*. So, with stomachs growling, they began the long, hard march through swampy paths which lasted the rest of the night and into the morning. But when they finally reached the train they found it had real compartments, with seats for everyone. And fresh air. This brightened the whole mood, despite their ever present hunger and thirst. The Ukrainians – or were they Russians? – gave them nothing the whole day long.

As the train got underway they beheld a landscape that had clearly suffered terribly during the war. Burned-out villages passed by on both sides; forests, fields, and meadows, all destroyed or damaged; and innumerable damaged tanks and other devices of war. There must have been a gigantic battle in this region. It seemed to Erika there had been no winners. Thousands must have died and given their lives for the madness of Hitler's idea of the struggle for power. How much misery this had brought on the families whose husbands, fathers and sons had had to fight in this war! She shuddered. Was this the reason the train was going so slowly, so that the German women would see and understand? Perhaps – though the state the railway tracks were in might have had something to do with it. The carriages were swaying like ships on a stormy sea.

Erika's eyes filled with tears. She imagined her father in a place like this. Would she ever see him again? As the train rolled on, one woman after another became lost in her thoughts, and a silent melancholy descended like a cloud on the passengers.

Evening came, and the train arrived at Kursk. At last, at one of the town's stations, they were given a portion of bread, dried meat and tea – not very much, but anything was better than nothing. Then, after a much needed toilet stop, the journey to Tula continued. Night now laid a welcome cloak over the misery outside, and soon it found its way inside as well, as one by one they fell asleep.

Around noon the next day the train stopped at a station in a larger town, which they guessed must be Tula. Sure enough they were soon ordered out and began to line up on the platform in rows of three.

Afterwards they stood in front of the station building and trucks came by to take them to the camp. Apparently the war had not reached this town. Was this still the Ukraine? Or had they reached Russia? Erika had as much of a clue about this as the rest of them – their geography just didn't extend this far. It was just one more town, with another camp, and yet more hard labour, harsh treatment, deprivation, sickness and misery.

They reached the outskirts of the town and, in the middle of endless farmland, they noticed a large area with several buildings in it, some low but a few quite tall, all painted in regulation Soviet dull grey. From a distance it looked quite peaceful and even friendly in the bright spring sun. The watchtowers told them it was their new camp.

The site turned out to be a large collective farm with its own internment camp. They could only see a few people working. It wasn't yet clear to the women whether this was a women-only camp, and whether there'd be more flesh-hungry guards to contend with, or just what kind of work the women would be expected to do.

A concoction of thoughts bubbled in Erika's mind. 'O God, please have mercy and help me here as well,' she prayed as she jumped down from the truck and lined up with the other women. There were a number of guards and other female personnel standing around looking bored. In the door of a smaller building with a tall chimney Erika saw a tubby-looking man wearing a light-coloured, dirty apron – evidently the camp cook had ventured out to see the new arrivals.

They had already been standing in the same spot for half an hour, some too weak to stand without the support of their neighbours, when at last the commandant appeared, an attractive woman in her forties, with a pretty face and long, blonde hair. Not so attractive was the malicious grin she wore as she eyed the German women while slowly walking past them. 'False as a snake,' thought Erika. 'Worse than Natali and Svetlana.' She breathed deeply – not least because standing still for so long made her dizzy.

The women were now treated to a long and rambling welcome speech by the commandant of this, the Pusstascha Collective. The commandant spoke German which, as she took great delight in explaining, she had learned during her years of forced labour in the German Reich, just as Svetlana had done. She was liberal with her terms of derision about the women, making it clear that they deserved captivity in Russia in compensation. She demanded unconditional obedience and the utmost discipline. Those women who got on with their work would get enough to eat. And whoever did not work would not eat. Shirking would be severely punished. Only the doctor of the military hospital could decide who was well and who was sick, who could work and who could not.

Then she told the women to go to the quarters assigned to them after roll-call. Every woman had to be ready for interrogation. And they were all to be back for roll-call at seven the next morning, when they would be assigned their work places.

Erika groaned inwardly. This commandant was going to be a monster – she was sure of it. Clearly it was her aim to give payback for all the difficulties she'd had to endure in Germany.

An hour went by, with no one allowed to move. Finally they were escorted by some women in uniform to their barracks.

Erika was assigned a place in a top bunk in the building next to the kitchen. The other inmates were apparently still out working somewhere. There was just one woman, lying on her pallet, unable or unwilling to speak. She certainly looked ill; her face looked old and grey; it was as if she had been poked by thousands of needles, or bitten by something. Were there vermin in this hole; was that why this poor woman was sick? They'd had lice in Charkow and there were bound to be lice here too. But Erika had never seen anything like this. It looked like the woman had been bitten by some flea-like insect far nastier than anything she had yet encountered.

At least there was something like a thin matress on Erika's pallet. It was filthy, but better to have this than sleep on the hard wood. Meanwhile her coat would serve as an additional blanket.

In the evening the women returned from their work in the fields. Like Erika and her friends they had all been shaved, though they wore scarves round their heads. They had been preparing the soil for planting, using just their hands.

It soon got noisy in the barracks, with much yelling, groaning and cursing. And then they discovered Erika. For a few minutes the new girl was the centre of attention. They all wanted to know who she was, where she came from, what she had done so far, how she'd endured the stresses and strains of her old camp, whether she'd been chosen yet for 'special services', and how many others there were with her.

Erika told them all she knew and in return asked them questions about camp life in Tula. 'All we know of this town is the station. But wait and see, sweetheart,' said a woman called Alice. By her accent she had to come from Saxony. 'I feel sorry for you – you're much too small for the work out there.'

Erika wasn't daunted. 'I've made it this far,' she insisted. 'I'll get along here as well.'

'The bedbugs will get along with you!' one of the women replied.

'I'm not afraid of them. They won't bite me,' she retorted. 'They don't like my blood. At least, I was never bitten by them in Charkow.'

'Well, they've sure eaten some of us.'

'What! Eaten you? They eat human beings?' Erika looked doubtful, but shocked.

'Sort of,' Alice confirmed. 'Some folk have already died. They bring all kinds of diseases with them. And if you're weak already . . . Look at Lene here – she'll be the next victim. She's not got long.'

'And if the bedbugs don't get you, then there's always the rats. They love warm human bodies, and they can get real nasty.'

'Ugh!' Erika shuddered. 'I hate rats.'

'They're not the only rats who like women's soft, warm bodies.' A young woman spoke, her voice filled with sarcasm and disgust.

'But the girl could be too petite for them,' added someone else. 'She's too tiny. The Russians love to get their hands on lots of flesh!' She flexed her hands to illustrate her point. Erika guessed she was trying to comfort her, but what the other women had told her made her shudder none the less. Then she told them, a little meekly, 'So far they've never picked me. Thank God.'

'Don't mention *him*. He's never shown up in this place,' someone remarked bitterly. No one else spoke.

'They used to choose by counting here too. But now they're less predictable,' Alice told her. 'They're choosing their victims during roll-call and then asking their colleagues where their sleeping places are.'

'Or they make us line up in front of our beds and walk through the barracks eyeing us up. When they choose one of us, they memorise the pallet number. Then, later on, they come back . . . None of us stand a chance.'

'And some of us don't even mind,' one woman added. But who she was talking about was not clear, and now the women were on to something else. Erika didn't get the chance to follow it up, as now the women were ordered to get their food. They all took their dishes and lined up to receive their share of bread – two thin slices – and one ladleful of cabbage soup. The procedure was similar to Charkow, and the rations tasted almost the same. Clearly they were standard provisions for German prisoners. The portions were not enough to satisfy most of the women. Because of her size Erika didn't need as much, but this wasn't enough even for her.

'They regulate the portions by ladle-size,' Erika was informed. 'Small ladle, little food; big ladle, more food. You're never given seconds. Whoever's caught cheating gets no food at all the next evening – no ladle, no food.'

'That *is* tough,' said Erika. 'In Charkow they were a little more generous.'

'If you want to survive here you'll have to obey, work hard and do whatever they ask you. Everything, girl, everything! Or else you'll not only go without food, you'll be in for the solo act or the wash-tub.'

'Solo act? Wash-tub?' Erika was curious. Did they get to perform here? Or maybe the washing facilities were much better than her previous camp? Unlikely.

Alice filled her in. 'Solo act, my sweet, means standing naked in front of everyone during roll-call and getting yelled at. Wash-tub means standing naked up to your neck in cold water for hours until you pass out.'

'That's terrible! Does it happen often?'

'Not if we can help it. But sometimes they're determined to have their performance, so they come up with some reason and choose a victim. Some have died.'

Erika felt a shiver run down her spine. Just at that moment somebody called her name: 'Erika Remplin?'

'Off you go for interrogation, little one. You're new here, eh? They just want to get to know you. It won't be that bad.'

And it wasn't, though it seemed to take for ever. Who was she? Where was she from? How was her health? It was very late when Erika returned to the barracks. The light had been turned off and, by the sound of it, most of the women were already asleep.

Erika lay down on her pallet and wrapped her coat around her. All of a sudden she felt cold, sad and scared of what was ahead of her. Thoughts ran through her head so fast she felt dizzy. She clutched her head.

How did she come to be here? What crime had she committed, that she should be taken off into the vastness of an alien land at such a tender age, to be exposed to the whims of these people?

And then, once more, she recalled her confirmation Bible verse:

> The Lord is with me; I will not be afraid.
> What can man do to me?
> The Lord is with me; he is my helper.[1]

---

[1] Psalm 118:6–7

At once the dizziness was gone and she was calm again. If what the psalm said were true when it was written, then it was true today. And how many times had she found it to be true already in her own experience? And so, comforted by the truth of those words, with her arms folded and a prayer on her lips, Erika drifted into sleep.

The next morning, in the cold before dawn, they lined up at the camp centre. The new arrivals were assessed for height and potential strength by the woman who had given the speech the day before, together with a man dressed in civilian clothes. Several guards stood around, looking bored as usual. The man in civvies was apparently the doctor, and he determined each woman's suitability for labour. Erika wondered what a doctor was doing here inspecting the workers, when quite plainly he should be looking after that poor woman in the barracks. But right now the living were clearly more important than the dying. The former did the work; the latter only caused it.

The inspectors stopped a moment in front of Erika, scrutinising this little person in her oversized overalls. An embarrassed, pitiful smile appeared on the face of the doctor, who was over a foot taller than Erika, as if to say: 'They should have left you at home, you poor, tiny creature.' Then he had a word with the commandant.

If only Erika had known a few more words of Russian, but she couldn't understand what they were saying. It rather looked as though the doctor thought this was no place for a petite person who was clearly not suited for heavy labour.

The camp commandant sent one of the other Russian women to the kitchen to get the cook, who was indeed the tubby little man they'd seen when they'd arrived. He bustled over, taking off his dirty apron as he came. The doctor talked to

him, pointing again and again at Erika. The cook looked at her
and nodded.

They seemed to have come to a decision: Erika did not have to
go out to the fields to work. She was to report to the cook after roll-
call and work in the kitchen. The commandant left Erika in no
doubt this was a special privilege which ought to be appreciated.
And woe betide if she should ever try to take advantage and abuse
her position.

After this the commandant and her troop turned to the
other newcomers and assigned them their roles. The women
were dispatched, though not without the odd cynical remark
aimed in Erika's direction. She, however, simply sighed with
relief and sent up another prayer of thanks.

The collective's new kitchen assistant hurried off to the appropriate
building to report for duty. Her first thought was how much
cleaner it could be, but already the rotund cook was welcoming his
new help with a '*Dóbraje útra!*' and shaking her hand, his chubby
face beaming. 'Igor. *Kak u-tibjá dilá?*' he asked, which had to
mean, 'My name's Igor, what's yours?' or possibly 'How are you?'

Using most of the little Russian she knew, Erika responded
with a smile: 'Erika. *Spassiba.*' But that was about it – and, anyway,
she didn't really want to tell him that she felt sick. Maybe it would
go away.

Igor ordered her to go and wash. Clearly it was important to him
that his assistant be clean, if not his kitchen. But what about her
clothes? They were filthy and stank. Erika signalled to the man with
gestures. He seemed to understand, but just shrugged, said something incomprehensible, and handed her an apron off a hook. That
was clearly going to be the full extent of the help he could give.

Erika went into the wash house to clean up her face and hands. This proved easier than in the previous camp due to the provision of something like hard soap. As for her clothes . . . it was going to have to get warmer first. She would need a warm spring day when she could watch her clothes dry as she lay in the sun. Hopefully her work in the kitchen would be seen to justify such a luxury. But for now . . . back to the apron.

Erika was soon given her first task: to get potatoes from the store room, wash them and peel them. Potatoes! The very thought made her mouth water. She'd have given anything for some boiled potatoes. (She knew only too well what raw ones tasted like.) 'Come on, girl!' she told herself. 'You're going to have to wait till you're back home. You're not going to get anything like that around here.' She walked around the outside of the building and downstairs into the store room. As soon as she opened the door she froze in terror. Her shrieking could probably be heard all over the collective. 'Help, Igor! Rats! Aagh! Go away, you horrible things!'

The little brown creatures obliged immediately of course, except that one of them lost his way and ended up in the trouser leg of Erika's overalls. This was reaching nightmare territory. 'Igor! Help! There's a rat in my trousers! Help!' She felt like fainting as she clutched the door frame.

The cook had heard Erika's yelling and was hurrying down the stairs. But too late. Erika had taken what action she could, and so the cook was met with the surprising sight of Erika in her underwear, her trousers round her ankles and a rat scurrying away. The flustered cook couldn't stifle the laughter that rose, though he slapped a hand to his mouth. '*Prastitje, prastitje!*' he snorted as he turned and disappeared back up the stairs.

Embarrassed but calmer now, Erika shuddered once more in disgust, pulled up her trousers and looked around the store room gingerly before filling her bucket with potatoes and hurrying back to the kitchen. Then she wiped away the few tears that she'd not been able to fight off. Igor, meanwhile, chuckled to himself.

'Rats . . . ugh! I hate rats!' said Erika, still flustered, as she heaved the bucket onto the table and looked for a knife. No sooner had she opened the drawer than she was shrieking again. 'Aagh! Cockroaches! This whole place is a *Prastitje*, Rats in the store room and cockroaches in the drawers! And I suppose there are silverfish in the flour too! It's disgusting – what kind of a mess is this, Igor? I want to go home!'

Igor came up beside her and looked over her shoulder. '*Prastitje*,' was all he said, and put his hand in the drawer. He took hold of the offending creatures, threw them on the ground, and trod on them. He shrugged his shoulders and simply said, '*Jest normalni.*'

'But this shouldn't be normal,' she replied angrily. 'This is a mess and it ought to be taken care of!'

Igor couldn't understand her words and only shrugged again, indicating that she should get on with washing and peeling the potatoes. And so they went back to work.

The days passed. Erika enjoyed her work in the kitchen with Igor well enough. He had clearly understood what had bothered Erika, and made an effort to clean things up. Every now and then he would even catch cockroaches as well.

But things were still bad, of course. Repeatedly Erika would have to make a fist in her pocket and swallow her anger, as her fellow countrywomen had to make do with dry bread and cabbage soup –

only occasionally replaced by *rýbni*, a thin fish soup, or *borschtsch*, a cabbage soup fortified with beetroot. And *káscha*, porridge, was even rarer. Meanwhile the Russians got to eat potatoes and rice, meat and fish, and a whole range of vegetables.

All the while Erika had to prepare such food without being able to eat it herself. Igor made sure she observed the rules, even if perhaps secretly he would have liked to let his little kitchen maid lick the spoon at times. But he had his orders, and they both knew full well that Erika had to resist all temptation, or risk being punished or even relieved from her duties.

By the same token she had to resist all requests by the others for extra food, even though she could easily have obtained it. But she did risk one thing. Whenever her boss was not around, and the ladles were spread out for the evening distribution of food, she would change the smaller ladles for bigger ones. Most of the time Igor failed to notice . . . of if he did, he said nothing. Perhaps deep inside he felt some pity for the German prisoners.

Clearly he felt for his kitchen maid: whenever Erika wasn't feeling well – which with her unbalanced diet happened a lot – he made sure that she was prescribed one or two days' rest. And on her return to work he always had something nourishing for her.

Erika wondered how she could demonstrate her gratitude. Igor had a wife who sometimes showed up in the kitchen looking for this or that. She was a nice woman. Erika thought about the nylon stockings her mother had put into her suitcase a year and a half before . . . Amazingly, through all the searches, they had remained intact. Maybe God had blinded their eyes, Erika thought, for just this opportunity. Surely Igor's wife would love to wear nylons? Erika decided to make him a proposition: nylons for potatoes.

Igor looked surprised and tried to grab them.

'*Njet!*' cried Erika. 'Hold on, my friend! *Potom!* Later! Nylons for *kartófil.*'

For a moment the cook looked like he didn't know what to make of this temptation. Then he glanced outside, as though making sure nobody was close by. '*Da, da!* All right!' He looked around one more time and motioned Erika into a corner of the kitchen where no one would see them, and then heaped several cold potatoes onto a plate. In return Erika handed him one of the stockings and set straight to eating the special delicacy. The taste! In her imagination she could even detect salt and butter.

She kept the second stocking.

Igor protested, of course, using several incomprehensible expressions. But she knew he'd grasped her intent. What good was one stocking for his wife? Erika had created a second opportunity. 'All right,' he capitulated. 'But be careful.'

Erika nodded. She knew not to risk losing her privileged position.

So far, Erika had always been spared when women were chosen for 'special services'. She reckoned that maybe one of the ways God ensured her protection was through the fact that she was simply skinnier than most of the other women. She was petite and flat-chested. What was it that one of the women had said? 'Russians want something in their hands,' – and Erika had little to offer in that department.

But the night finally came when one of the Russians had decided to break with custom. Quietly he slipped into the barracks and found his way to Erika's bed. And now there he was, hands wandering underneath the coat that served as a blanket, underneath her very clothes. At first his victim slept on, unaware of his lust. But when she felt his hand on her chest, she woke up startled.

She wanted to scream. Immediately her attacker held his hand over her mouth. Then she heard the harshly whispered command which all the Russian men seemed to know in German and which all their victims had come to dread: 'Come with me!' Erika panicked. She tried to fight her way out of his grasp, but he held his tiny victim under his arm such that she couldn't move or make more than muffled sounds.

Even so, it was enough. Several women woke up. One of them was Alice, the 'boss'. As soon as she saw who tonight's victim was, she groaned, and then shouted out, 'Take your dirty hands off her – she's just a girl! Go find some other victim, you–!'

At that very moment the door was opened and a name was called into the darkness: 'Erika Remplin! Go at once to interrogation!' The intruder released his grip, cursed silently, and rushed to hide from his colleague behind the door. Erika struggled forward, saved on the very brink.

When it came to interrogation, Erika was getting quite canny. The sessions always seemed to happen at night, but the Russians didn't appear to be following any kind of system. Some women were not questioned for several weeks; others were summoned almost every other night. Maybe it had to do with the prisoners' history – some of them had held important positions in the Nazi regime. As for Erika, apart from her membership in the BDM, she was too young to have any kind of political track record.

When she lay back down on her pallet later on, Erika considered how God had rescued her through the amazing timing of her interrogation. 'God, you are mighty. You're really powerful and strong,' she prayed. There and then she renewed her vow to learn more about him as soon as she was home again. She prayed that that would be soon!

Meanwhile patience was called for. Time passed slowly for Erika, and then she developed a strange sickness, apparently caused by an abscess on her left leg.

It began as a small spot on her shin. She even thought it amusing at first, with a hair right in the middle of it. It began to itch, and she concluded she'd been bitten by a bedbug. But her symptoms weren't right. Then the spot started to hurt. Her temperature went up, till it was plain she had a fever. The thing started to grow bigger and bigger, and soon looked like a little volcano on her skin.

She felt sick, though she still went to work. You couldn't just 'call in sick', and at roll-call it was hidden from the doctor under the trousers she wore.

It was Igor who noticed that his assistant was not well. Her face was very pale and drops of sweat covered her face. 'You not well?' he asked her, concerned.

'No, Igor, I feel terrible,' Erika admitted, as she came over dizzy and grasped hold of the table.

'What is matter?' he asked. Erika answered by showing him her leg.

'*Jest furunkul.* Doctor! Now!' Igor took off his apron, hung it up, took Erika's hand, and led her across the square to the military hospital unit in one of the barracks. Erika had never been here before. It looked quite clean, though before she could take a good look round Igor marched her straight into the examination room.

The nice doctor she knew from the roll-calls examined the thing on her leg and came to the same conclusion as the cook.

'*Jest furunkul,*' he told her, and reached for a bottle with brown liquid which he dabbed onto the abscess. The tincture caused a stinging pain. But then Grandma Luise had always said, 'Fight fire with fire.' So Erika clenched her teeth as she tried to decipher the tag on the bottle. 'Iodine' it said – by now Erika knew most of the Cyrillic letters and in this case the letters were the same as in western Europe.

The doctor exchanged a few words with the cook before he called for a nurse. The woman knew a little German and translated the doctor's orders. Erika was to stop working right away and lie down. There was room here in the military hospital. The leg had to be exposed to the sun during the afternoon. Erika could sit out in the sun, while Igor was to brew her some special tea and give her vegetables for lunch. Each morning she was to be treated with iodine, and each night ointment would be applied. This way the abscess would break open within a few days, the pus would ooze out, and the whole thing would heal soon afterwards. However, she still had to line up with the others each morning at roll-call.

What in any normal situation would be pretty unwelcome news filled Erika with joy. This was like a holiday. She would get to sleep properly, she wouldn't have to work . . . she'd even get to relax in the sun! She'd be able to wash her clothes and get them properly dry. She would get to eat special food – solid vegetables, not the cabbage soup they'd all become so tired of. She would eat bread and drink tea. And she would have a few days to herself, without the usual gossip and, more importantly, without the danger of being selected for 'special services'.

Of course there was bound to be talk each morning while they lined up. Some of the women made it plain how much they envied Erika her sickness and her special treatment; others called her a dosser and a skiver, and said they'd see about getting her some 'special treatment' all right . . . Erika tried not to let it affect her and told them to go find their own abscess – maybe then they'd feel better!

After a few days Erika was able to resume work in the kitchen and continue her battle against rats, cockroaches and silverfish. Once more she had to prepare good food for the Russians which she herself was denied. But Igor grew a little more generous by looking the other way and letting her take the leftovers.

'Just as well,' thought Erika, 'now all my nylons are in his wife's drawer.'

CHAPTER 7

Coming Home

During the summer of 1946 Erika had to endure several more abscesses. The days when she was off sick all followed pretty much the same routine. She welcomed the treatment, but became progressively weaker. Her work became more difficult, and she longed for her captivity to end. Why didn't God answer her prayers now? Why did those disgusting things continue to appear on her leg? And all the time she had to listen to the women's silly talk.

Autumn came, and early one chilly morning, much to the amusement of the guards, all the women were told to line up naked. It was Erika's birthday. She stood there with the others, shivering with cold and embarrassment.

At last the 'flesh inspectors' turned up, the key one clearly being the doctor. While each woman's name was read out he looked closely at her and allocated a number. The women then had to gather in groups according to their number. Erika was assigned a number 4, along with the other weak or sickly looking ones. As she joined them, she wondered what kind of orders would follow.

They soon got their orders, though things were far from clear. The women of Group 1 didn't have to go and work out in the fields – they had one hour to pack their belongings and get ready to leave. The commandant said nothing about where they were going, which left the women feeling uneasy. All they knew was that after the harvest and during the winter not many workers were needed at the collective. Perhaps they were going back to the woods. Nobody spoke.

The women of Groups 2 and 3 were to get ready for work. They were staying and would continue to work for the Russians and do whatever else was required. Their resentment was plain to hear.

The women of Group 4 were to get ready for work as well and meet back at the same place. Erika was confused. Why divide them into a group of weaklings if they had to work like the others after all? Clearly something different was going to happen to them, sooner or later. Once more uncertainty and lack of information became cruel weapons in the Russians' hands.

Erika could scarcely understand her own feelings when, that cold day in October, she waved goodbye to the women of Group 1. Where they were headed nobody knew, though no one thought it was home. Those women were too healthy and were bound to be useful somewhere else. Meanwhile Erika had to remain at the Pusstascha Collective, wondering whether her time in the kitchen was coming to an end. Igor didn't know – or didn't want to say – and Erika took to praying with a new intensity over the days that followed. She begged God to have mercy and put an end to her misery.

Four long weeks later Erika and the other women in Group 4 were ordered to a special roll-call. It was the evening of the 26th November 1946, and some twenty women stood there in the cold snow wondering what kind of news was coming. And then the moment arrived.

The commandant appeared. In serious tones she spoke about the generous Russians who had so openly given the German women the opportunity to make amends for the cruelty that their fathers, husbands, brothers and other German women had done to countless Soviet people. She said it would be more than appropriate that the women show their gratitude to the Russian workers and guards of the Pusstascha Collective. They had let them work and treated them most humanely. The fact that some had not survived their time here was an unfortunate tragedy. Those who had survived would probably have to work much harder once they were back home . . . to rebuild the lives and the society that had been destroyed by the madness of the insane German Führer.

Once they were back home . . . Erika was sure she had heard those words. But the commandant droned on. 'It is a good thing that that monster, the Führer, is no longer among the living. But it is a shame that he has escaped his responsibility and left his people to themselves. Still, at least many of his accomplices have been called to account and sentenced to death; and others will spend the rest of their lives behind bars.'

At this point the commandant paused – presumably for effect, though nobody responded. The women were freezing and eager to hear what the commandant was building up to. And so she continued: 'You will be given your discharge papers and permission to travel home. Tomorrow morning a truck will take you to the station in Tula. From there you will go to Moscow and then further west. On behalf of the Pusstascha Collective I wish you a safe journey and an enjoyable return.' Then, with an ironical 'So long and goodnight!', the woman brought her speech to an end – sarcastically, for sure, but no less welcome for all that! She handed the women the papers they had dreamed of for so long, and dismissed them.

The cold was forgotten – nobody moved. Good news was warming them like a glowing hearth. They stood there, papers in their hands, unsure what to make of it all. Suddenly one woman gave a cry of joy, and the tension broke. Some of them hugged each other, others wept for joy, while still others stood there, speechless.

One more night and they could go home! At last!

Erika felt that her eighteenth and nineteenth birthday celebrations had come at last, and more; and to celebrate she did something she had not done in all that time – she danced. She danced like a ballerina – at least as far as her impractical clothes allowed. She danced almost as she had danced before, in another world, another time. She may have looked crazy as she danced across the square, holding the discharge paper VI/948 with pointed fingers just like a veil, but off she went, finishing in front of the commandant with a small pirouette and then kneeling, tilting her head. Tears of joy were running down her pale cheeks.

The Russian officer seemed moved. '*Spassiba*, little dancer,' she smiled, and reached out her hand to the young ballerina, pulling her up as she said, 'Thank you. Once again, safe journey!' Just then Erika felt like giving her a hug.

The next morning after breakfast their journey began. The women had even been given some extra slices of bread – a secret leaving present from Igor.

But bread was not the only thing that slipped in unnoticed: doubt was not far behind. Could they really be sure they were going home and not just to some other camp? Could they trust the commandant's words? And so a gloom descended on the train compartment, as they sat, tired and weak and unable for now to give up the fear that had become part of their lives.

What finally helped them was the change in the alphabet on the station signs. Cyrillic gave way to more familiar characters, and they realised they were travelling through Polish territory. As before the country was covered in deep snow. More relief flooded their hearts after the train crossed a large river and the names of the towns started to sound German. Still they were restrained and quiet for the most part. Their destination remained unknown, and the conductors still spoke Russian.

By now the train was definitely on German soil, and they were surprised to see the conductors pull the blinds down. Now what were they trying to hide?

There was no answer as the mobile cages rolled on. The uncertainty lasted another day. First they felt the vibrations of a lot of shunting and coupling, as clearly a new train was being put together; then the journey continued, though in which direction no one could tell. It remained dark in the compartment, and although they tried to peer through a little opening behind the blinds they couldn't see anything that told them where they were or which way they were going. But after a few more hours the brakes squealed and the train came to a halt. They could hear voices outside, both Russian and German ones.

German voices! Had they reached their destination? Where were they? Erika had a window seat so she pushed the blind aside again. 'We're in Marienborn,' she told the others. 'Does anybody know where that is?' Nobody did – it had to be a small station. No answers yet.

Just then the compartment door was opened. Two men in different uniforms entered. One of them had a pistol on his belt. The Soviet stars on his fur cap and coat lapel spoke for themselves. The other man seemed to be from the German Railways rather than the military. Clutching a folder he had brought with him, he welcomed the returning women in German. 'Good evening, ladies. Welcome to Germany!'

Erika soaked up his words like a dry sponge in water. It was unbelievable, like waking from a nightmare. The man was still speaking. 'You are in Marienborn, at the western border of the Soviet occupation zone. May I see your papers please?'

What was this? The Soviet occupation zone? They were nonplussed by the term . . . were there Russians inside Germany? And if there was a Russian zone, would there be a British one, or American? Suddenly fear returned . . . the fear that, even now, they had not escaped the Russians.

The women took out their Russian discharge papers. The Russian man took them first, examined them closely and handed them on to the German who then compared the documents with a list he'd taken out of his folder. As he gave them back to each woman he asked where she wanted to go. And so the list went on: Hamburg, Lüneburg, Stendal, Kassel, Stuttgart . . . Each time he checked a different list, telling the woman whether she should leave the train or remain on board. He then made a note on his list.

'Why are we being separated already?' Erika asked him.

'Well, young lady, those returning to places situated in the Russian occupation zone stay on this train and go back to Magdeburg first.' He told Erika which towns this applied to. 'From Magdeburg connecting trains will take them to their destination.'

'And the rest of us?' queried the 'young lady'.

'You will cross the border to the British zone on a different train. It's the one on the other platform. Others will look after you in Helmstedt. Wait and see.'

'Is it a long way to Helmstedt? We're hungry, and we've not even had a drink since yesterday.'

'I'm sorry,' he said. 'It isn't too far away, but you'll have to wait a bit longer for the train to leave. I'll have to ask you to get off this train now please. And, again, welcome to Germany and have a safe trip home.' With that he stepped out onto the platform and then entered the next compartment, accompanied by soldiers who had been waiting outside, to repeat the procedure with the other ten women from the Pusstascha Collective.

Inside the compartment the women began to say their goodbyes. Tears flowed in the wake of the many long months of shared suffering which, in spite of differences in age, outlook and character, had bound them so closely together. For now their paths parted into the unknown – until the border between the occupied zones became a national border. Already they seemed to sense that this would not be an easy border to cross. Nobody thought to exchange addresses – not that they had a single pencil or piece of paper between them.

Erika joined the women in the other compartment to say goodbye. What would become of them all? Would they meet again some day? And what was waiting for them back home?

'It's all in God's hands,' said one of the women who was travelling to Chemnitz. Erika had never met her at camp – more's the pity, she thought.

One hour later, the train comprised of just two carriages arrived in Helmstedt in the British zone. Nobody boarded to check documents. In the end one of the women opened the door and immediately they heard the loudspeaker: 'Welcome home! Welcome to Germany! Welcome to Helmstedt!'

This time the tears were tears of joy.

There were crowds of people waiting on the platform. Women wearing Red Cross insignia came to the train doors and helped the women to disembark. Others took their luggage. Everywhere people were hugging each other. Erika stood there, taking it all in, and let the emotion wash over her.

It was a while before she noticed the British soldiers. Suddenly she shrank back from a black man in a uniform who was reaching out his hand to her with a broad smile: 'Welcome to Germany! Welcome, little *Fraulein*. Now that you're back in *Deutschland*, *alles* will be *gut*. God bless you!'

Funny way of speaking, thought the 'little Fraulein'. He pronounced the *r* as if he had a hot potato in his mouth. Potatoes! Erika's stomach gave a sudden rumble . . .

There were no potatoes immediately forthcoming, but their surprise and joy knew no bounds when they were served hot chocolate and white bread in the heated waiting room. Such delicacies! Erika closed her eyes as she sipped the delicious steaming liquid. And the bread! She didn't know anything could taste so good. Next came a piece of chocolate – over an ounce of real chocolate! What a welcome-home present!

It all seemed so unreal to Erika. Only a few days before she had been hundreds of miles away in the east among Russians, having to endure the cold and dark, hunger and want . . . not to mention constant cynicism all around. And now she was back home in Germany in this unfamiliar city with the British, surrounded by warmth and light, friendliness and compassion. God, how great you are!

For this surely had to be God's doing – had he not answered her prayers? And the prayers of two of the women from Chemnitz who'd been singing Christian songs on the way? It was an Advent hymn,[1] and she recalled some of the lines. It went, 'I lay in fetters groaning' but when 'He comes, all grief and anguish shall at His Word be still'. She'd found the last verse particularly moving:

> He comes, the Lord, to judgement;
> Woe, woe to them who hate!
> To those who love and seek Him
> He opes the heavenly gate.

When it talked about an opening gate it surely didn't mean the barrier you could see here at the station . . . yet in some way this was a gateway to heaven. The sheer warmth, and light, and friendliness – all the delights of this welcoming hour. Truly she had come home.

Those two friendly women must have been in other barracks, and of course she herself had not worked out in the fields. She was sure she could have been friends with them. She sat on her case and mused about what it would have been like to have known them in captivity.

Suddenly Erika started. She must have dozed off – the voice of a woman wearing a British uniform was bringing her back to reality. She introduced herself as 'Second Lieutenant Ann'. Another welcome was followed by deep regrets for all the misery the women had had to suffer in the Soviet camps. 'From now on, the *Zeit* will be *besser* for you,' she told Erika and some others in the same mix of German and English as her colleague's. 'Sadly I must limit your happiness a little,' she went on. 'First, you'll have to go to a hospital,

---

[1] 'O how shall I receive Thee?' Original by Paul Gerhardt.

a *Krankenhaus* – you'll be in quarantine till you've been examined. Then we'll have to see about getting you home.'

Her words were unbelievable.

'But you can write letters in the meantime. We'll help you with that.'

Erika's mind raced. The world was changing fast.

'Later you'll take a bus to the hospital, but before that we'll have to make lists and register all of you. So please, *kommen Sie*, one at a time.'

The registration was carried out quickly and soon they were sitting in an English military bus, being cared for by women from the Red Cross. They crossed the city which, as far as they could tell in the evening light, had not been affected much by the war. Here and there they saw Christmas decorations.

Erika closed her eyes and pictured the last Christmas tree she'd seen, back in Gosslershausen. She had squinted at it so that the candle flames looked like little stars. She could smell the aroma of roast goose that Grandma Luise had prepared; she could taste the cookies and the roast apples.

> O Christmas tree, O Christmas tree,
> How lovely are thy branches . . .

A year ago there had been no Christmas. No one thought about celebrating love and light in Charkow. Christmas wasn't kept in the Soviet Union anyway. The only winter joy for the prisoners had been an additional ladle of soup because of the frost in January. And that was it.

How would it be this year . . . Christmas at home? And where was home? Erika pondered this as the bus swayed through the streets. Wasn't home where her family was? But where was that? She had to find out over the coming days. The counsellors were bound to help her, and she needed a destination address whatever happened.

What about Hörde? Had her father returned and rebuilt their house? And her mother? Had she been able to leave West Prussia and get back to the Reich? But there was no Reich any more! Only Germany, defeated.

Erika knew that she had to get a grasp of the new situation. The coming days and weeks would need to supply a lot of answers.

She woke when the bus jerked to a halt. She'd been dozing again, and dreaming. It took a moment to get her bearings, to remember she was back in Germany, in the British zone, in Helmstedt under the protection of the English and the Red Cross.

Still a little sleepy, Erika followed the others off the bus and into a building with the red cross above the entrance. This had to be the hospital where they were to spend the coming days. It was a comparatively luxurious hostel, with bright rooms for six people each. There were nice beds with soft matresses and clean bedding, all in rooms that could be heated. Each patient was given a cabinet where they could put their belongings. Inside Erika found a simple nightgown and two sanitary towels.

Erika took them both out, and sat there looking at them. She wondered when her last period had been. As she thought back she realised she'd not had a single one for the entire two years in camp – nothing since she'd been at home in Gosslershausen. She recalled many of the women complaining that they had no way of sorting themselves out. Erika had been spared two whole years! Right now that felt like a special gift from God, in line with his promise, 'The Lord is with me; he is my helper.' Her heart was filled with thanks.

Before they went to bed they were given a meal with tea that tasted like tea, plus some bread with real cheese. But that wasn't all. They could now use a real toilet and have a wash before going to bed, even drying themselves with a clean towel.

As Erika lay down she meant to pray, but the exertions of travel and the excitement of the last few hours took her straight off to sleep.

The next few days in the hospital were characterised by examinations of various kinds, and treatment, lots of questions, writing letters to relatives and civil authorities. In their free time the women relaxed their aching bodies and simply enjoyed themselves. Here among the British and the Red Cross they could breathe and speak freely. They were finally able to read a newspaper and learn about the new world, or read a book. At night Erika soon came to lose the fear that someone might come for 'special services'. They were free and they were safe. It was almost too much to take in.

Erika made the most of the next few days, especially as she seemed to need less care than many of the other women. She helped to make Christmas decorations, read stories and sang carols. She succeeded in finding the complete words to the song the two women had sung on the train, 'O how shall I receive Thee?' Up to now this song had been unfamiliar. What was it supposed to mean, Erika wondered, as she read the words again?

> Love caused Thine incarnation
> Love brought Thee down to me;
> Thy thirst for my salvation
> Procured my liberty.

Clearly the hymnwriter was saying something about God loving us – loving her, Erika – so much that he was 'brought down' for her. She read on:

My soul puts off her sadness
Thy glories to proclaim;
With all her strength and gladness
She fain would serve Thy Name.

That made sense. The hymnwriter was so grateful for God's love that sadness had to make way for service in the future.

Even so, right now another thought was on Erika's mind: would she dance again?

And sadness didn't look ready to depart just yet. The day before Christmas Eve Second Lieutenant Ann arrived with bad news. 'The city of Dortmund is not currently granting entry. I'm afraid there's no address for you, and no work. What do you want to do, *Fraulein* Erika?'

This was hardly the Christmas present she was hoping for, and she couldn't help but show her disappointment. 'I don't know,' she said eventually. 'What about our house in Beukenberg Street?'

'It's not habitable,' replied the lieutenant in the best German she could muster. 'Still *kaputt*. Do you have another address?'

Erika thought for a moment. Then she suddenly cried, 'My aunt Erna and her daughter in Bochum! I used to live with them for a while. Perhaps they're still there. Maybe Wiltraud can help me get a job. Then I'd have an address *and* work.'

'Sounds like a good idea. Why don't you write a letter straight away? There's paper in the office.'

So there was to be no 'home for Christmas' for Erika. Apparently none of her family had reached Hörde yet. Still, maybe her plan with Aunt Erna would work out.

While she waited, she joined the Christmas celebrations laid on for them. It was a truly international celebration, complete with sparkling Christmas tree and the Christ-child in the manger below.

They sang German and English carols, and the Christmas story according to Luke was read to them in both languages. Then the same black English soldier she had seen on her arrival got up to say a few words.

'Twenty months ago Germans and English considered each other enemies. But now we celebrate Christmas together, the birth of the Saviour of all mankind, Jesus Christ. What a gracious God!' He clasped his hands together, and went on to say that this was possible because God still loved his people and had not given up on them. The holy child in the manger was a sign. After a brief life among men, he had become the man upon the cross, and three days after dying he had become the man from the empty grave. He had been born, had lived and died, and then been raised to life for all people, so that everyone who believed in him would be set free from their sins and have eternal life.

Everyone listened intently as the young soldier spoke. God had permitted this war with its terrible outcome. Why? That was so very hard to understand. But it didn't change the eternal truth that God wants peace for his people. This is why he sent his own Son Jesus, the Prince of Peace, and laid him in the manger. 'We won't know peace in our own hearts, or peace between people, or peace between nations, without this Child of Peace. Whoever wants this kind of peace needs to accept this holy child. And so, once again, this Christmas is an invitation to give your heart to the babe in the manger, and to give him central place in your life.'

With a joyful 'Glory, Hallelujah! Amen!' the man ended his speech. Erika could see she was not the only one impressed.

Afterwards presents were handed round: new stockings, a nice set of underwear for each woman, some biscuits and a helping of punch. Pure delight.

It was the turn of the year: 1947. Despite the celebrations all around, Erika had gone to bed and slept right through. The medical examinations and interviews were now a thing of the past – Erika was pronounced severely underweight but otherwise physically sound. They told her to take care of herself, though there was little chance of a diet approaching anything anyone would consider normal. Food was rationed in the whole of the British zone, which encompassed the entire Ruhr district including Bochum.

The other official pronouncement was that Erika would be subject to no special denazification procedure. Her membership in the BDM was not of itself deemed sufficient cause.

So now, with the year still new, the nineteen-year-old Erika waited for a destination. And in the third week of January the long-awaited answer from Bochum arrived. In addition to some hearty greetings from Aunt Erna the envelope contained a permit to enter the city and a labour permit from a company Erika didn't recognise. She wasn't told what she'd be doing, but all that mattered was that she could now move on. What came after that . . . well, she would see soon enough.

The time came for goodbyes. 'To you nice English people, I say *da-swidánija!*' Erika announced with a smile. But then she immediately corrected herself. No Russian – never again. Better to say, '*Auf Wiedersehen, liebe Freunde.*' For that's what they had become – dear friends. Not only the friendly soldier who had dubbed her 'little Fraulein', or Lieutenant Ann; everyone had treated her courteously. Erika had no doubt that the British would have had good reason to behave differently towards the Germans after what the Hitler regime had done to their country and their citizens. Yet clearly these people from across the English Channel took a different view from those in the east. And, who could say? Perhaps there was a desire deep down to make up for the severity of their retaliation against Germany's provocation. If that were true, then thank God for it.

Maybe it was coincidence, maybe it was destiny; but on the 21st January Erika received her ticket from Helmstedt to Bochum – the very date on which, two years earlier, she had been forced to travel east. But this time her direction was west, homeward bound. She couldn't help but wonder whether God was reassuring her. As the British soldier had said, he guided the destinies of nations and of individuals.

As Erika made the difficult journey from Helmstedt to Bochum, on crowded trains and with multiple changes, she thought about the soldier's words. Somehow she knew he'd been right. She had never heard the Christmas message like this before. They had had a Christmas tree at home and in Gosslershausen, but no one ever talked about who the child in the manger was. There had been no room for this message about the Saviour of all mankind in their 'German Christian' family. It was only at Aunt Erna's that Erika had come to know a little about the God of the Bible. After that she had often thought about him, and over the many times she had experienced his help he had become more and more important to her.

Yet she knew she had not given him a place in her heart. Perhaps now, somehow, he was showing himself to her in a new way. Faith had taken root in her heart. Would it have room to grow?

CHAPTER 8

Working on the Farm

The reunion at Aunt Erna's was filled with joy. They talked for most of the night about the events of the last two years in Bochum, in Gosslershausen, and in the Soviet camps. Both of them wore their coats against the clinging cold in the room. Erika learned that her mother had also been deported somewhere into Russian territory, but so far nobody knew where that was or whether she was even alive. Erika could not hold back the tears – her poor mother; she was bound to be worse off than Erika had been. Greta had been a fervent party member and office-holder within the Women's Movement.

'We don't know,' Aunt Erna consoled. 'But we can pray that God will protect your mother as he has protected you.'

Erika also learned that, when the war was over, her father had been interned by the Americans for a while and then returned to Hörde. There he had cleared their place out and rebuilt the ground floor to a habitable condition. Then he had left to work on a farm in Paderborn.

Grandma Luise and Erika's brothers and sister were still in a detention camp in Poland. Luise had written to say that they would be released soon and that she would like to live in Hörde with the children. But she needed permission to return from the city of Dortmund.

'It's likely that Grandma will have to wait,' said Erika sadly. 'I didn't get permission for quite some time. Oh, I can't wait to see them.'

'Be patient, Erika. You'll see them soon. Luise's got the children with her, so the authorities will be more lenient. Meanwhile you stay here for now. You're safe here. And in a few days we'll go and see my doctor. He needs to take care of you before you get any thinner. You're so bony, you poor thing!'

'But I have to work for this company . . .' she objected.

'No, Erika, you don't. You can't work when you're so under-weight. No, no. And the work permit's a fake anyway. They issue them so that the city can grant entry. It was Wiltraud's doing, you know.' (She didn't, but she was impressed.) 'I'm sure the doctor will come up with a different recommendation.'

'And what will he say?'

'He'll probably say you'll have to gain a few pounds before you can work anywhere!'

'But how am I supposed to gain any weight with a food short-age on?'

'I know,' said Erna. 'And it's true, it's particularly bad here in the cities. It's terrible how many people are starving here. The occupying forces are doing their best to get more provisions, but they can't turn stones into bread, and unfortunately quails and manna don't come falling from heaven these days either. The people out in the country are better off.' She thought for a moment. 'Yes. We'll find somewhere for you in the country – maybe even somewhere close to your father.'

'That sounds good. But right now I'm happy to stay with you and Wiltraud.'

'You won't see her much. Ever since she's been working in Düsseldorf, she only comes here for the weekend, if at all.'

'What's she doing in Düsseldorf?'

'She's working for the new government of North Rhine-Westphalia.'

'North Rhine-Westphalia?' Erika was astonished. 'What's that?'

'It's the name of the new state that the British occupation has set up here.'

'It seems quite a lot's changed over the last few years, Aunt Erna.'

'Quite a lot, my child. But you'll get the hang of it all soon.'

'I suppose I'll have to learn a lot of new things all over again.'

'But not today!' Aunt Erna objected with a smile. 'Let's turn in. You're tired from your journey, and I'd like to go to bed too. Tomorrow we'll have to see about getting coal from somewhere, or else we'll freeze to death and won't even be able to warm soup up. This winter's too cold.'

Erika said nothing about the cold, but she wondered where they'd get coal from.

'Well,' said Aunt Erna, 'one thing's for sure. We won't be doing it the way a lot of people do.'

'And how's that?'

'They jump into passing coal trains, fill their bags, and throw them off at certain points. That's stealing. It's not for me.'

'But how are we going to get any if we don't steal it?' Erika asked gently.

'We'll pick up the pieces that fall on the ground when they load up at the goods station and when the lorries drive off. The workers often turn a blind eye if people gather then.'

'Then can I take a bucket as well? Maybe we'll be able to fill two.'

'Very well,' Aunt Erna smiled at her great-niece's offer. 'Would you like to hear the Bible reading for today?'

'Why not?' Erika replied. 'Do you still read the Prussian Text . . . or whatever it's called now?'

'What do you mean? Why should it be called anything different?'

'Well, if this state isn't called Prussia any more, shouldn't it be the North Rhine-Westphalia Text, or something?'

Erna took it all rather seriously. 'But that doesn't mean the name of the Bible version has to change. The word of God never changes! It stays the same even if the conditions in this hard world change. So, I'll read to you Psalm 86. That's the reading for tonight.'

'May I read it? I've never read the Bible out loud,' Erika offered.

'Then it's high time you did, my child! Of course you can.'

Erika began to read, utterly astonished at how this ancient psalm seemed to speak about so many things from her own life – her past, her present, and maybe even her future.

> Hear, O Lord, and answer me,
>> for I am poor and needy.
> Guard my life, for I am devoted to you.
>> You are my God; save your servant who trusts in you.
> Have mercy on me, O Lord,
>> for I call to you all day long.
> Bring joy to your servant,
>> for to you, O Lord, I lift up my soul.
> You are forgiving and good, O Lord,
>> abounding in love to all who call to you.
> Hear my prayer, O Lord;
>> listen to my cry for mercy.

In the day of my trouble I will call to you,
> for you will answer me.

Among the gods there is none like you, O Lord;
> no deeds can compare with yours.

All the nations you have made will come and worship
> before you, O Lord;
> they will bring glory to your name.

For you are great and do marvellous deeds;
> you alone are God.

Teach me your way, O Lord,
> and I will walk in your truth;

give me an undivided heart,
> that I may fear your name.

I will praise you, O Lord my God, with all my heart;
> I will glorify your name for ever.

For great is your love towards me;
> you have delivered me from the depths of the grave.

The arrogant are attacking me, O God;
> a band of ruthless men seeks my life – men without
> regard for you.

But you, O Lord, are a compassionate and gracious God,
> slow to anger, abounding in love and faithfulness.

Turn to me and have mercy on me;
> grant your strength to your servant and save the son of
> your maidservant.

Give me a sign of your goodness,
> that my enemies may see it and be put to shame,
> for you, O Lord, have helped me and comforted me.

Psalm 86

Silence filled the room in the wake of Erika's voice. At length,
after she had returned the Bible to her aunt, she spoke. 'That's a

wonderful psalm. It's almost as if David knew my life. There are so many things that fit perfectly.'

'That's how it usually is. God's word mirrors human life – whether we believe or not.'

'Maybe I don't yet, fully,' Erika responded thoughtfully. 'I think I'll have to take this one verse and make it my prayer.'

'Which one?'

'The one about the way. Please read it to me once more.'

'I'll read it as our evening prayer.' Erna read verse 11:

> Teach me your way, O Lord,
>   and I will walk in your truth;
> give me an undivided heart,
>   that I may fear your name.

'Amen. And now, off to bed. We can talk about it again tomorrow if you want.'

The days that followed were spent trying to get their daily bread and finding a way to heat the house. It was not easy to get domestic fuel. The little amount they got with their ration coupon was nowhere near enough for that winter. And the coal they were able to pick up didn't help much either. There were just too many people.

By day Erika gazed at the frost patterns on the windows. In the evenings the two women sat at the table, with their coats on, reading or talking.

They talked about spiritual things a lot, which Erika knew was doing her good, but somehow it didn't really touch her heart as yet. It was going to take more time. But Aunt Erna was not the kind of person to put pressure on someone. She knew that Erika had to understand for herself, that her belief in God's mercy needed to travel from her head to her heart. She committed Erika to God.

The visit to the doctor turned out as expected. Erika was to go to the country as soon as possible, where the nutrition would be richer and provide more fat. This 'little doe' needed to put on weight as soon as possible. He suggested that her father might find a place for her in the Paderborn area – though the work was not to be too hard. Domestic work would be best.

After the examination Erika sat down and wrote a letter to her father in Bentfeld, near Paderborn. And after four long weeks of waiting she received his answer. He told her that there was a farm in Elsen, a village close by, where they needed help. Erika was to start working there in March. There was just a farmer's wife there, with her two children and an older girl who helped out. The farmer was still at a British dentention camp. Her father had already made the arrangements. Erika was to live on the farm and her main responsibilities would be the house and the children. The other girl mainly worked outdoors.

Her father closed his letter by saying that, if she took the job, they'd be able to meet up every now and then, as his work was not too far away. He was looking forward to seeing her again.

The next day Erika made enquiries at the station and found out that Elsen was between Dortmund and Hannover. So once more she packed what little she possessed, ready to begin a new chapter in her life.

'We'll keep in touch, Aunt Erna. And thanks again for everything.'

'Remember, your confirmation verse is just as true in Elsen! And don't forget your evening prayer, child – you know, the prayer from the Psalms. It's where you marked the text in the Bible I gave you. God be with you!'

Erika nodded, though her heart was filled with the sadness of parting, albeit mixed with growing excitement about what lay ahead. She couldn't wave from the train because it was heaving with people, large suitcases and bags strewn everywhere. She stood out with her small suitcase and the well worn shoulder bag that dangled loosely around her body.

In Dortmund Erika had to wait more than an hour for her connection, so she used the time to visit the area just outside the station. She wept as she saw the devastation brought by the bombs of the Allied squadrons. It made her want to go back to Hörde to see her parents' house. But she knew she didn't have the time. And maybe it was better that way; there was enough misery here.

Before long she was on the next train, standing squeezed between people with brimming bags and cases. At each stop some more got off, until finally she was able to sit down and rest her short legs.

A lot of people got out at Paderborn. By now Erika had learnt where all these people were going. They were on their way to the rural areas to exchange various bits and pieces from their urban apartments for food – sheets for sausages, tablecloths for bacon and cheese, china for potatoes. How many hearts were bleeding as they gave up their precious items only to fill their stomachs for a few days? And what about those people whose belongings had been buried under the ash and debris? How did they cope?

As she journeyed on her mind turned to her own situation – how much food would there be at the farm in Elsen? She would love to eat a real meal again. To feel full again . . .

After another hour she was standing at last in the village centre. In front of her was the farm gate. It was shut. Erika hesitated. What was waiting for her on the other side? Whom would she meet and would she be welcome? What kind of work would she have to do?

'Come on, Erika,' she said to herself quietly. 'The Lord is with you to help you.' Hadn't Aunt Erna reminded her of this very promise before she'd set out?

She took a deep breath and then pushed open the little door within the gate. She walked into a roughly cobbled yard surrounded by buildings. Farming tools were left on the ground and a large dunghill was steaming, sharing its odour generously. A few chickens ran away at the sight of her. On the left side of the barn there was a large dog barking. It looked dangerous, though it was on a leash. She immediately resolved to make this monster her friend as soon as possible. Then a horse whinnied in the stable directly across the yard from her. So far she couldn't see anyone.

Dutifully Erika closed the gate behind her and looked around again. Then she glanced across to the main house to her right just as the door opened. A girl who looked about seven leaped out. She had blond pigtails and was wearing a colourful dress. As she smiled she gave Erika a good view of spaces between her teeth. 'Be quiet, Hasso!' she shouted at the dog. Then she stopped in front of the stranger.

'Are you Erika who wants to work with us?' Before Erika could respond she added, 'Your daddy was here.'

'You're quite right,' laughed Erika. 'I am Erika. And who might you be?'

'I'm Margret. I'm already seven and I'll soon be going to school. My sister's name is Inge and she's ten.' The girl had already taken Erika's hand and was pulling her towards the house. If everyone on this farm was this nice then Erika knew she'd be just fine.

Suddenly there was an older girl holding out her hand. With disarming candour she said: 'Hello, Erika. I'm Inge. I'm almost as tall as you are and I'm only ten. And Gertrud's much taller than you!'

Erika laughed. 'Yes, unfortunately I was made a little short. You're not the first to notice! But I have a big heart for little girls who are as nice as you and almost as tall as me. And I don't have a problem with people who are taller than me either.'

'That's good,' Inge said. 'You can put your bags in the hallway. We'll take you to Mummy and Gertrud. They're in the barn feeding a calf. It was born this morning, you know. Have you ever held a calf? It's *so* amazing!'

A few moments later Erika was standing with the two girls behind seven cows and watching the farmer's wife and Gertrud try to get the little calf to feed from its mother. The little speckled animal still seemed a bit clumsy.

Eventually, the woman got up, wiped her hand on her apron and held it out to Erika. 'Welcome to the Göbel-Heinemann Farm, Erika Remplin. I hope we'll get along well – all five of us women.' Then Gertrud also shook Erika's hand. She really was tall, and sturdy too. Erika noticed how big her hands were – and what a grip! Like a sailor, she thought.

In fact Erika was nearer the mark than she could have guessed. Later on, as they sat around the kitchen table, she learned that Gertrud's brother was skipper on a boat on the Rhine in Duisburg. He was waiting for permission to work again. Their parents were both dead. It seemed that Gertrud wanted to work on the boat as well. But until the authorisation came through she was happy to be at the farm and to have work. Housework definitely wasn't her thing, so she was more than happy not to give up her milking pail and pitchfork for the washboard and wooden spoon!

'Excellent – we complement each other then!' said Erika, very satisfied with this division of labour. 'I don't know if I'd be able to hold a pail between my knees, and pitchforks are way too heavy for me. Plus, if I'm honest, I'm a bit scared of large animals. And as for insects . . . I think they're disgusting! So give me the washing and the cooking – if there's anything to cook, that is . . . I certainly got some practice in the Soviet camps.'

Ouch – she'd said it, and now it was out she had to tell them more of her story. She knew she couldn't go over all the memories, still so painful, so she gave them a shortened version. Even so, it gave her the opportunity to say how God had protected her from many evils, and how he had guided her home again.

The two children seemed particularly stirred by Erika's words. 'Here you won't have to be afraid of anyone! Not rats or cockroaches! And not Hasso either – once he knows you he'll be very friendly.'

'And you won't get overworked here,' the farmer's wife put in. 'Kitchen, living room, children's room – these will be your work place, and kitchen utensils and cleaning equipment will be your tools. And it won't be long before you get some meat on those bones again. We'll try and feed you up a bit.'

'I can't remember the last time I was full,' Erika whispered, looking at the ground.

'Don't worry! As long as we have food and the occupation don't confiscate everything, we'll make sure you get more than the prescribed 1200 calories a day. You won't starve here.'

Another friendly person, Erika thought – even though this poor woman had had to live without her husband since the end of the war. As a leading farmer he had been detained by the British. He'd told them he'd done nothing wrong – just propagated some of the Nazi slogans among the farmers and put some dissenters under pressure. He knew he'd been mistaken even as the Allies bombed his beloved Paderborn. And now he counted himself fortunate that that minor leadership role had spared him from fighting at the front. And as it was, he reckoned that the occupation forces wouldn't hold him for ever.

That night when Erika went to bed she felt content. She had at last been able to eat her fill and drink fresh milk. And, after all this time, she had got to sing her special lullaby at a child's bed: 'Heidschi, Bumbeidschi . . .' Margret had particularly enjoyed it.

This was the first evening in a while that Erika looked forward to the next day. So now she didn't neglect her evening prayer:

> Teach me your way, O Lord,
>   and I will walk in your truth;
> give me an undivided heart,
>   that I may fear your name.
> I will praise you, O Lord my God, with all my heart;
>   I will glorify your name for ever.
> For great is your love towards me;
>   you have delivered me from the depths of the grave.[1]

The tiny plant of faith was growing.

That spring was the start of a good year in Erika's life, the best so far. She had her father nearby and was able to share some happy moments with him. She felt at ease in the farmhouse. She got on well with the farmer's wife and her two girls, and connected particularly well with Gertrud. She soon became friends with Hasso too, and she got more and more used to the work she had to do. As time went by she put on weight and became stronger, and so her interest grew in the other areas of work on the farm.

She decided first to take a look in the barn, but without going anywhere near the horses. They were too tall and too strong. The pigs weren't so dangerous, but she couldn't stand their discordant

---

[1] Psalm 86:11–13

squeals of hunger. The chickens and the ducks were funny enough, as they came flying whenever anyone approached with a feeding dish, but she had to watch out for the geese, which would often hiss viciously and stretch their necks menacingly. If that happened she simply had to confront them in a resolute manner. Fortunately she saw no rats on the farm. They did have some mice but they were rather cute and hardly ever showed themselves anyway.

Erika was enthralled by the cows. Even though they were tall they were really gentle, warm and soft creatures. She would have liked to have a go at milking one of them – it would make a change from the house work. But up to now only Gertrud and the farmer's wife got to do it.

The time for a change came in the autumn when Gertrud went back to Duisburg to work with her brother on the boat. Erika offered to try milking. The farmer's wife agreed and had more than one laugh at Erika's expense as she tried in vain to get the milk to come. The beasts were just not interested. But she kept going, and they came round in the end. Maybe it was something to do with the cheery song she whistled or sang as she came into the barn? Yes, that was it. 'Cows love music,' she announced to her new admirers.

One of the reasons for Erika's happy mood was that she now weighed more than eight stone again. The downside was that, slowly but surely, the few clothes she possessed were getting too tight. She could hardly buy new ones, with not a penny to her name.

Then she had an idea. At one of their meetings her dad had told her about a relative who lived in America. Maybe she could tell her all about her plight – after all, wasn't everyone agreed that Americans were rich people who could be relied on to send what people were calling care parcels? So she asked her father for the address and wrote a long letter to Aunt Toni in Cleveland on Lake Erie in the state of Ohio. She told her a little about herself, since the poor lady probably wouldn't know who she was at all, and described her situation in great detail – carefully including her dress size and height.

A few weeks later Erika thought Christmas had come three months early. The twenty-year-old received a large and heavy parcel, stuffed full of coffee, rice, corn, sugar, chocolate, peanuts, stockings (apparently handmade), lace underwear, a woollen nightgown, a bright red dress, and a pair of elegant heeled shoes. Erika was amazed. It was as if the gifts had come from heaven! Lord, you're with me to help me! It seemed it paid in all kinds of unexpected ways to trust in God and to count on him for help!

And, lo and behold, she found that very sentiment expressed in the letter enclosed in the parcel. Aunt Toni said that the most important thing in life was to trust in God's promises and to rely on his grace, as the writer of Psalm 118 clearly knew. She had written a verse from the psalm:

> It is better to take refuge in the Lord
> than to trust in man.
> It is better to take refuge in the Lord
> than to trust in princes.[2]

Aunt Toni was surely right. She was even right in her comments on recent German history, Erika decided. It had taken such an evil and lamentable direction simply because so many people had relied on a self-appointed 'prince' who could not endure a God who was higher than him. She wrote that she hoped the German

---

[2] Psalm 118:8–9

people had learned their lesson from those events and would never let it happen again.

Erika sat at the table with all the things spread out before her and re-read the letter several times. She recalled how her confirmation verse also said she should rely on God. She resolved to read the passage again in her Bible, realising with some shame that she turned to it rarely. That had to change. But then she'd decided that so many times before! Perhaps God would help her in this matter as well.

In the late autumn of 1947 the farmer returned from the British camp. His wife and children were naturally overjoyed. He was a handsome man, but taciturn. But then, as Erika thought about it, she realised he had spent months in the company of only men and without anything to do. And doubtless he was still absorbed by his past. Now, as he faced work on the farm with four women around – the three youngest of whom were very spirited – it was bound to take him some time to adjust.

By Christmas most of the tension of adjustment had eased and they were all set for a peaceful holiday season. They almost forgot the child in the manger, but Erika made sure that the 'holy infant so tender and mild' was not forgotten. She asked to read the Christmas story from Luke Chapter 2 and from Matthew Chapters 1 and 2. It might be a Catholic house, and not yet Epiphany, but they were going to hear about the wise men at Christmas!

The farmer agreed and so for the first time in their lives Margret and Inge heard what Christmas was really about, beyond the tree whose evergreen branches delighted them so. Erika began to sing an old Christmas carol with a sweet Sicilian melody:

> O how joyfully, O how blessedly,
> Comes the glory of Christmastime!

To a world so lost in sin,
Christ the Saviour enters in:
Praise Him, Praise Him, Christians, evermore!

O how joyfully, O how blessedly,
Comes the glory of Christmastime!
Jesus, born in lowly stall,
With His grace redeems us all:
Praise Him, Praise Him, Christians, evermore!

O how joyfully, O how blessedly,
Comes the glory of Christmastime!
Hosts of angels from on high,
Sing, rejoicing, in the sky:
Praise Him, Praise Him, Christians, evermore!

Johannes Daniel Falk & Heinrich Holzschuher

The whole family were clearly moved by Erika's reading and singing. For them, as for so many, the actual meaning of Christmas had been lost under National Socialist ideology. Now, at their first Christmas celebration together after the downfall of Hitler, the wonderful message of the birth of the Saviour was heard.

Did this Christmas Eve awaken memories of past times for the farmer and his wife? Surely, thought Erika, Christmas still had some meaning in Catholic homes. Would it surface again in German society over the coming years, now that Nazi propaganda had failed so completely? Time alone would tell.

Either way Erika herself had discovered afresh the wonderful truth of the old Christmas story. That speech by the British soldier a year before had doubtless paved the way. She recalled it vividly as she lay in her bed that night and reflected on the last few hours.

The joy she felt over this day, the family celebration, the presents she'd received and the few she was able to give (thanks to a second parcel from Aunt Toni) made Erika's heart swell with gratitude.

And now a new question came into her mind, one that surprised her: when would she be able to celebrate Christmas with a family of her own? With a loving husband and children? How amazing that would be! She reckoned it was unlikely she would ever be able to celebrate Christmas with the whole Remplin family, now that they lived in different places.

And still there was no word about her mother.

But it was all in God's hands – this she now knew. And he knew the answer to her questions . . . even the one about a husband. He'd need to show up, for starters!

'Please, Lord, let me meet the right one,' she prayed as she fell into a calm and deep sleep.

CHAPTER 9

A Surprising Encounter

The winter days were busy, but everyone got on well as they carried out the daily routine. Rural life still suffered from the occupation. The only time they met other people from Elsen was when they worked outside the farm, or when they went to run some errands in the village, or when another farm worker came by. There were some children who often came to play with Inge and Margret. Erika would have dearly loved to meet people of her own age, not least some younger men. But it seemed it was not to be – not unless God had other ideas.

In the spring of 1948 there was more work to do in the fields and meadows, so the farmer went looking for help. His first idea was to find another female worker to help his wife, but out of the blue a young man showed up.

He was tall, with dark, wavy hair. Erika watched him standing awkwardly, holding his backpack in his hand and looking lost. Not very impressive. She calmed Hasso down, approached the stranger and held out her hand to him. 'Hello, I'm Erika Remplin. I'm the housekeeper.'

'Hello to you too. Otto Wolzak. I'm supposed to be the farm labourer here.' He was clearly mimicking her rather curt style, hardly able to stifle a grin.

This did not go unnoticed. 'Carry on grinning, Otto Woolsack, or whatever your name is. Not everyone can be as tall as you are. Physical height is not a sign of greatness, you know.'

It was a fair cop. 'Sorry, Erika Rempel, or whatever your name is. I won't grin again. But you just look so funny in your colourful dress and your frilly apron.'

'Erika Remplin, if you please. As for this – it's all the rage in America. Better frills than fringes; better colourful than patched,' she replied with mock offence and an unsubtle reference to the young man's own attire.

'Hmm, sorry about that. Unfortunately I don't have anything better. My name's Wolzak, by the way, not Woolsack. Is the farmer about?'

'All right, Otto Wolzak. But I'm afraid you'll have to wait a while. The farmer and his wife are out in the fields.' She looked down a moment. 'You are in the right place, I suppose?'

'Why shouldn't I be? Or is this not the Göbel-Heinemann farm?' A flicker of doubt crossed his brow.

'It's just that, well, we're waiting for a female assistant. But you don't look too female.'

'Indeed. Last time I looked I was still a man.' Erika coughed. 'I was told to report here. That's why I'm here.'

'All right. Wait here,' Erika ordered. 'The farmer will have to sort this out.'

'What is there to sort out? Don't you think I'm fit for work?' Otto asked with raised eyebrows.

Erika gave a little laugh. 'It's not a question of whether you're fit. There's only one room for the servants. And I live there.'

'So what? All you'd have to do is budge up and there'd be room enough for me,' Otto teased.

'You wish! You are a rascal!' Erika was outraged.

'Sorry for the third time. I didn't mean it like that. But I do need to know . . .'

'Why don't you take a seat on that bench over there. Or you can go and clear out the barn if you like. You'll find the tools right next to the door. You'll find the dunghill, I'm sure. The farmer and his wife will be here in an hour. Meanwhile I've got work to do in the house.'

She left him in the courtyard and went back to work in the house. Weird guy, she thought. She could have done without an amateur. Then again . . . she could see through the kitchen window that the amateur had actually put his backpack on the bench and was already mucking out the barn.

Maybe not so bad.

When the farmer and his wife got back from the fields they decided that although Otto was not what they'd ordered, now he was here he should be given work. His pre-emptive barn-cleaning had impressed them – he seemed to be someone who saw the work, had enough strength, and was not afraid of a bit of dung!

They solved the accommodation problem by converting a small store room. They cleared it out and then put in Gertrud's redundant bed and cabinet. Everyone was happy.

Otto at home on the farm in West Prussia in 1941.

At dinner they learned that Otto was twenty-five and came from a devout Protestant family. He would have liked to return home to West Prussia after his brief spell as a prisoner with the Americans, but he'd been turned down and so needed a place to stay. With the help of a friend he'd ended up in Paderborn and had found work on a farm in another village nearby. When the farmer there had returned from detention with the British, Otto was no longer needed. So he was only too pleased to be here now. 'I hope I can become a part of the community here – even though I'm not a girl . . .'

This last comment warmed things up nicely, and soon they were all engaged in lively conversation, Margret and Inge playing a full part. The little one was her usual direct self: 'Otto, will you marry Erika?' Poor Margret didn't understand why she got a telling off from her parents after that. Erika blushed.

Hoping Otto hadn't noticed, she quickly changed the subject, seeking urgent clarification on tomorrow's division of labour. After dinner the farmer took young Otto aside and began to introduce him to his new responsibilities.

Later in her room Erika thought about Margret's question. Why had she asked that – was she just being cheeky, or was it prophetic? Could this man be God's answer to her prayers for the right husband? As she thought about it, she decided no, probably not – he wasn't really her type. He was much too rigid and awkward. Definitely not. Then again . . .

He'd said he came from Freystadt. That was a small town situated on the railway between Gosslershausen and Riesenburg. She'd been there once with her family. It was a beautiful place, near a lake, with a historic monastery and a large Protestant church with a tall tower standing at the end of the market square.

And he said he came from a devout Protestant family. She wanted to talk to him about this some more. Why had he mentioned it? 'Dear God,' she prayed, 'if Otto really is the one, then please give me a sign.'

The new band of workers got on well. Otto soon proved an able and diligent worker who could be employed anywhere on the farm. He was clearly not as clueless as his young colleague first thought. Affable and pleasant, he was willing to work and very courteous – not least when he and the physically weaker Erika were working together.

But he knew how to tease – and Erika was often his target. He hardly ever walked past her without undoing her apron strings. At other times he would hide her tools, or leave a mouse that the cat had caught in front of her door. Then later, to make up, he would leave a flower in the same place.

He was clearly attracted to Erika. Whenever it was possible he tried to be near her. At first she repelled his advances, but as time went by she softened, and the two of them could often be seen sitting together out in the yard after they had finished their work. They would talk about God and the world, about their past, and their hopes for the future. Their individual pasts were very different, though they did have some things in common: prison camp was prison camp, even though Otto wouldn't begin to compare his time with the Americans to her time with the Russians.

Their dreams for the future were similar: a family, children, a profession with civilised working hours and a decent income, a little house and a garden . . .

'Well, in that case why don't we do it together?' It was a lovely evening in early summer, and Otto was risking all.

'What's that supposed to mean?' Erika objected. 'That's a crazy idea!'

'Well,' Otto persevered, 'I was thinking that you and I would make a nice couple.'

'Well, you may think so,' she retorted. 'But we are nothing – and we have nothing. Where would we live? And how would we make a living, Otto Wolzak?' She turned away, then said more calmly, 'Anyway, I'm too small for you. Put it out of your mind.'

'But I don't want to, Erika Remplin,' he came back stubbornly. 'You said yourself that physical height had nothing to do with greatness. You're perfect for me. I just . . . like you.'

'Okay, you like me. That's all well and good – but do you know if I like you?' she pouted.

'I'd like to know, my little colleague. I hope I didn't do all this hard work in vain?'

Erika looked at him with big, quizzical eyes. 'You know, I thought you were a kind and courteous person. But I see now you're just a big egotist whose only concern is his personal and domestic future dreams.'

'That's rubbish! You've got it all wrong!'

Erika changed the subject. 'You said when you arrived that you're from a devout Protestant family. Do you believe in God?'

'That's a weird question,' Otto said, looking unsure.

'But it's important to me,' Erika insisted. 'I need to know.'

'I'm not sure,' he admitted. 'At home we used to read the Bible and pray regularly. Not just before meals as you do here. Faith has always played a central role in my family. "Jesus Christ is King" was one of my parents' favourite songs. They lived what they believed. We children all went through confirmation . . . though I can't remember my verse any more. The Hitler Youth made us all forget our beliefs – not that that was difficult in my case, since my faith wasn't really established. It was only later that I discovered their arguments against the Christian faith burst like bubbles; but by then I didn't really care.

'So I can't answer your question with a yes or a no.' He hesitated, clearly lost in his thoughts. Then he looked at her. 'What would be your answer? Do you believe in God and Jesus and everything?'

Erika looked down at her hands and said quietly, 'I want to believe. I know that God is there. I've experienced his help so many times at camp, during the long journeys, and even here on the farm. My confirmation verse is true – the Lord was with me and he has helped me. And I want somebody to share this belief with. It would make things easier – hence my question.'

Otto studied her face. Could it be that her response did not mean rejection? He took up her silent question. 'Then let's try to believe in God and Jesus together,' he said cautiously. 'Do you own a Bible?'

'I do,' she said, but then admitted she hardly ever read it.

'Then let's read it together. I haven't got one. And who knows? Maybe this'll help our faith grow.'

Erika brightened. 'So . . . when do we start? Today?'

'Today's fine by me!'

Moments later the two of them were back on the bench and reading some verses from Mark – chosen because it was the shortest of the Gospels. They read about the heavenly voice which said to Jesus: 'You are my Son, whom I love; with you I am well pleased.' Then they went on to Jesus himself saying, 'The time has come. The kingdom of God is near. Repent and believe the good news!'[1]

'This is so hard to understand!' Otto moaned. 'Repent and believe the good news? We need someone to explain this to us!'

'But there's no one here. They're all Catholic – they don't read the Bible at home. In fact, there isn't even one on the premises, apart from mine. The priest at church is the only one who reads it.'

'In that case,' said Otto, affirming his intention to keep going, 'we'll just have to find a way to interpret it.'

Suddenly Erika remembered something. 'Aunt Erna always said that we need to pray to God for the Holy Spirit to help us understand the meaning.'

'Then we'll try that. And maybe we'll understand a bit more as time goes on.'

They remained on the bench until late that evening. In the end the farmer's wife had to interrupt them. 'Tomorrow's a new day – and the night will end at five o'clock!'

They didn't get to read the Bible every day, but more and more they found the time to read Mark's Gospel. They were astonished at what was written about Jesus – his words and his actions. But often they'd have to stop to get on with their work. As time went on they inevitably drew closer together. As Otto

---

[1] Mark 1:11, 15

increased his attentions Erika became more open, both roman-
tically and spiritually.

One day the two of them were alone in the meadow, working in
the hay. When they got to their break they started playing about
and chasing each other across the field like care-free children. At
first he ran after her, then she chased him, and so it went on.
Finally they lay in the hay, laughing and giggling. Otto decided to
stop her laughing with a kiss.

Erika's first thought was to object, but she was so happy she
gave in. Her first kiss! It was a moment of pure joy. They both
remained sitting in the hay and held each other's hands.

'Do you remember when we first met?' Otto asked her.

'Mmm . . . clueless guy laughs at little person . . .' Erika
recalled.

'You just looked so funny with your American dress. And the
frilly apron! But one thing was clear to me right from the start.'

'And what was that?'

'I knew I'd like flirting with you.'

'I thought you were awful at first – the way you stood there, stiff
as a broomstick, with your frayed trousers and your patched jacket.'

After that, Erika let the kisses keep coming.

That afternoon made things clear to them. They knew they
belonged together, and they would stick together, come what
may. Erika knew that Otto was God's answer to her prayers. Otto
had not prayed for this of course, but was equally sure she was
'the right one'.

But what would others think?

Erika knew she should tell her father as soon as possible. She
rode her bike over to where he was working and told him about
her relationship with Otto.

'Before you get engaged you must introduce me. I want to take a look at my future son-in-law first!' he demanded.

'He's a decent man, Papa,' Erika assured him. 'I've been praying for the right one and God has sent him to me.' This remark seemed lost on her father, though he looked satisfied.

'I don't object to your relationship. But remember: you're not twenty-one yet.'

Erika saw the need in him to have the final say. 'Don't worry, Papa. We're in no hurry.' With these words Erika got on her bike again and rode back to Elsen. In the evening she announced to Otto that his future father-in-law wanted to meet him.

'Then let's go and see him on Sunday,' Otto suggested.

The farmer – who was still catching up with his wife, to whom all of this was no surprise – then chimed in. 'Okay, you can go on Sunday as soon as you've finished work. But please be back in time for barn duties.'

The two girls already considered it a done deal – at least, Margret did. 'I knew it! I knew Otto would marry Erika!' she exclaimed over dinner with a broad grin.

The young couple tried to downplay things a little. 'First of all we'll get engaged, Margret,' Otto explained.

'The wedding will come later,' Erika added.

'Will you still live with us on the farm? Or will you live in your own house in the village?' Clearly Margret for one was planning ahead.

'They don't know that yet!' put in her mother sternly.

'No – we haven't even thought about it yet,' Erika confirmed. 'First my father has to give his permission for Otto to be my husband.'

'And what if he says no?' Inge asked seriously. 'He doesn't know Otto, after all.'

'Yes, sweetheart, then what?' Otto moaned with mock sorrow.

Erika waved him off, and then came up with her solution. 'In that case we'll wait till the 21st October when I'm twenty-one. Then it's up to me who I marry!'

'Daddy, will I be able to marry who I want when I'm twenty-one?' Margret asked.

'Oh, we'll see – if you bring the right man home, why not? But there's plenty of time before then.'

The eight-year-old seemed satisfied with this response, and they all continued with dinner.

Two days later the couple cycled over to see Erika's father. Otto was dressed in his best trousers and shirt. Thanks to the wonderful summer weather there was no need for a jacket. Erika was wearing a stylish new dress which Aunt Toni had sent her. Otto was sitting on the saddle of the old boneshaker, pedalling as hard as he could. Erika sat side-saddle between his arms on the crossbar.

They were cycling along the paths between the fields, singing happy songs. They stopped in the shade of a hedge, held hands and squinted into the sun as they watched a buzzard circling ever higher with two of its young. They were absorbed in thoughts of their own family. What was Erika's father going to say?

They looked down, only to see smaller creatures cavorting around their feet. Wonderful nature!

'God saw all that he had made, and it was very good,' Erika quoted solemnly.

'Ah . . . from the very beginning of the Bible – and it's meant for you and me, my darling,' Otto replied. 'But we'd best get going. Your dad is probably waiting for us.'

They pressed on, and were doing so well until a large stone got in their way. With Erika sitting in front of him, Otto couldn't see it coming. When the front wheel hit it Otto lost his grip on the handlebars. At once he lost his balance and they both landed in the ditch.

'Aagh! My best trousers! And look at my shirt – ruined!'

'What about my dress?'

'True, but you don't have to impress your father. I do!'

'Don't worry about it, Otto darling. It's the inner man that counts,' she soothed.

'Hmm . . . well let's hope your father's a good judge of character then!' He sounded doubtful.

'We'll soon find out.'

They checked the bike was not damaged and continued. A little later the hopeful couple stood in front of the man who could become Otto's father-in-law – if he wanted to.

'No, this is simply not possible!' exclaimed Erika's father as they approached. He exploded with laughter. 'This is the Otto who wants to marry my Erika? Unbelievable!'

Erika did not understand. Otto's eyes bulged.

Erika and Otto shouted their responses at exactly the same time: 'You know Otto?' and 'Erika is your daughter?' They looked at each other, astonished, while Arthur Remplin was convulsed with laughter.

'Is someone going to tell me what's going on here?' Erika demanded.

'All right, I'll tell you,' answered Arthur. 'Otto, Erika is my daughter, and I believe I can entrust her to you.'

Erika still looked puzzled.

'Dear girl, I've known Otto for quite a while! We've had breakfast together several times now.'

'Breakfast? Where? When? I think you're making fun of me.'

'No we're not,' her father retorted. 'You see, the fields which belong to my farmer and the ones that belong to yours have a long common boundary, with just a hedge in between. Well, Otto and I have often found each other ploughing by that hedge at the same time – hence we ended up having breakfast together! And getting to know each other. See? And yes, he's all right – you may marry him.'

It took a few moments for Erika to take it all in, especially the last part, but then she threw her arms around her father and kissed him – something she hadn't done in years. Then she hugged Otto and kissed him as well. Finally she drew a deep breath. 'I can't believe it.'

'I think we should celebrate this moment and have a toast,' said her father. 'Hang on a moment – I've got some brandy in the larder. I'll go and get it.'

As he went Otto kissed Erika again. He was so happy. 'Erika, we *shall* be husband and wife – and with permission!'

Erika freed herself from his arms. 'But let's not rush it. First we'll get engaged, and then married. Let's say we'll get engaged on the 21st October, and then get married in May next year.'

'Why then?'

'Well, I turn twenty-one on the 21st October. So we'll have two things to celebrate, which will save money. And the merry month of May is just the best time to get married. Don't you agree, Otto Wolzak?'

'I agree, Erika Remplin. You'd better start practising your new name – I don't want you accidentally pronouncing it "Woolsack"! And we'd better get saving.'

'Yes, and don't forget – "every little helps". So remember to put coins in the money box. Now, time for the toast.'

'No sooner said than done!' Arthur was back and handing his two children a glass of brandy each. 'Here's to you both!'

Erika was about to repeat the toast when suddenly her tone changed and she said, 'No, here's to Mamá and the children. Let's hope they all make it to the wedding.'

'Quite right, my child. That's our hope. To Greta and the children!'

'Then we should pray for this,' Otto put in. 'With God all things are possible.'

Erika took one sip of the brandy and shuddered. Then she said: 'The second toast is to us. And that's the last – this stuff knocks me out!'

'Just as well you only have to drink such a toast once!' her father commented.

'True,' she said seriously. 'There won't be a second occasion.'

'I should hope not!' put in Otto, who then suddenly remembered the time. 'Hey, we'd better get going. I can almost hear the cows moaning!'

'I told you Otto's a good man!' said Arthur. 'You'll do all right with him.'

'Do all right? He throws me into ditches!' joked Erika. 'Thanks, Papa! See you soon!'

And off they went, the happy couple, as if they were literally riding into their future together.

On their way Erika reminded Otto of his idea of praying for her family to be reunited. 'Did you just say it, or did you really mean it?'

'Sweetheart, I meant it! God can make it happen by the wedding in May. You pray for it, and so will I. And then we'll see how God can help.'

'Do you know this makes me love you even more, Otto?'

'Excellent. Hug and kiss to follow as soon as we're home!'

The following weeks on the farm were idyllic for the young couple as they looked forward to October; although one little dark cloud did cross their horizon briefly.

The farmer was in the fields with his two workers and the horse-drawn wagon, ready for harvest. It was Erika's job to arrange the sheafs on the wagon to fit in as many as possible. Otto's job was to hand her the sheafs using a three-pronged pitchfork. The accident was naturally a shock to everyone. Whether Otto swung the fork too high, or Erika slipped because the horses started, no one could say; but suddenly a cry was heard from the top of the wagon: 'Otto! What are you doing? You're not supposed to spear me with that thing! Help, I'm bleeding!'

Otto and the farmer looked up to see that two prongs of the pitchfork had speared Erika's left thigh. Quickly Otto threw aside the fork and clambered up into the wagon, leaping like a monkey to help Erika. She was sitting among the sheafs, holding her leg which was bleeding freely.

'Couldn't you be more careful? Look what you've done,' Erika groaned.

Otto looked helpless and guilty, and tried to console her: 'It was an accident . . . I can't see you down there. I'm so sorry, darling. Let me take a look at it.'

'Take your hands away,' she cried. 'It hurts!'

'I know. But you need to get down. Come on, I'll help you. The farmer will carry you. He'll know what to do.'

Very carefully, Otto took Erika by the hand and helped her off the wagon. The farmer took hold of her. 'Ouch, that hurts!' she cried again.

'It looks worse than it is, girl. It's only a flesh wound. Fortunately there's a lot of muscle in the thigh. It will soon heal.'

'And what do we do now?' Otto asked as he climbed off the wagon.

'The two of us will load the rest of the harvest onto the wagon. Then you carry Erika home. Take the shortcut. My wife will be able to see to the wounds. We won't need a doctor. It's not as bad as it looks.'

And that's what they did. The two men finished loading while Erika sat in the stubble and waited. She gritted her teeth as she held her leg. Then Otto lifted her up and carried her home.

Erika soon forgot her pain as the ambulance turned into a joy-ride.

'Do you know why I speared you, darling?' Otto asked as he finally set down his burden on the bench at the farm. Then he delayed her answer with a kiss.

'Yes. Because you are a villain, using methods like that just so you can carry me in your arms! Now, call for the farmer's wife so that she can take a look at the holes you've made.'

Moments later the woman examined Erika's wounded thigh. Her two daughters looked on with interest. Unfortunately, Otto couldn't stay because he was needed elsewhere. The last thing he heard was Erika yelling, 'Iodine! Ugh! I hate it!'

The farmer's wife used a wad of cotton soaked in iodine to clean the wounds. 'Why does it have to burn so much?' Erika moaned quietly.

'Fight fire with fire,' the farmer's wife replied, before applying some ointment to the wounds and bandaging the leg.

'Just what Aunt Erna used to say,' commented Erika and gritted her teeth again.

'I think you'd better take two or three days off and rest your leg,' said the older woman. 'You'll soon be better. Margret can keep you company. You can practise reading together. Inge will have to help me.'

Erika was content, and even grateful to Otto for the short break. She would make good use of it to think about their future together.

CHAPTER 10

Gifts from God

The engagement party was planned for three months' time, in Elsen. The only thing they didn't know for sure was whether the celebration would be on the farm or somewhere else. It was to be a Thursday, which was fine by the farmer. Planning the event had become easier ever since the currency reform in June, when the Deutschmark was introduced – at last the shops were selling items that nobody could hope to buy before. And the things Erika received from Aunt Toni helped her with bartering. Coffee for this and cigarettes for that, a piece of cloth that was too large for one that was perfect . . . and so on.

The weekend before the engagement the two lovers sat together one last time to consider their future together. They wanted to be absolutely sure before they exchanged the rings which, although made of cheap metal, had still cost them several pounds of coffee and several cartons of cigarettes.

'I've found some words in the Bible that fit you perfectly,' Otto told her.

'Read them to me,' Erika suggested as she snuggled in close. Otto opened the book of Proverbs and read: ' "He who finds a

wife finds what is good and receives favour from the Lord."
That's chapter 18 verse 22. Or here's chapter 19 verse 14:
"Houses and wealth are inherited from parents, but a prudent
wife is from the Lord." '

'Thank you, my darling. I don't reckon either of us will inherit
much – but the other bit's good! I'm happy if you find something
good in me, consider me prudent, and if you can see me as a gift
from God. And I hope you'll always receive favour from the Lord.
I've found a verse, too, by the way.'

'Then read it to me. Did you read the book of Proverbs as well?'

'I did. You can find great things about me in chapter 31! Okay,
here goes. It says: "A wife of noble character who can find? She is
worth far more than rubies." Verse 10.'

'Very nice. It's an amazing gift from God that you are to be my
"noble wife" in every way. I'm sure I'd have found it hard if you
had to tell me that the men in the camps had done to you what
they did to the other women.'

'You don't know how many times I've thanked God for his
protection from those awful men! But look, there's more here.
Shall I read it?'

'Go ahead,' Otto replied.

Erika read the next couple of verses: ' "Her husband has full
confidence in her and lacks nothing of value. She brings him
good, not harm, all the days of her life." Sounds good, doesn't it?'

'A wonderful prospect for a husband-to-be,' Otto agreed.

'There you go again, rushing ahead,' teased Erika. 'Engagement
first, remember; and with God's help we'll make it through – and
then we'll be ready for marriage.'

'You're a sweetie, and Solomon really was a wise man,' Otto
intoned as he took the Bible again. Erika looked at Otto lovingly

and expectantly as he read from the end of the chapter: ' "Charm is deceptive, and beauty is fleeting; but a woman who fears the Lord is to be praised." ' Then with a grin he added, 'But I've got one who has all three – charm, beauty, and the fear of the Lord.'

'I think God's going to have to help me with the last one.'

'Sure,' said Otto, 'but what does your verse say again?'

'The Lord is with me to help me,' Erika quoted the concise version.

'There you are – it's in your verse. God himself wants to help you – and me too, I hope.'

'Hold me, my darling, and tell me you love me and that we'll never, ever part, no matter what happens.'

'Why are you crying, sweetheart? What is it?' There was a glimmer of fear in Otto's voice.

'Nothing, it's just that I'm so happy, and I'm not used to it. Though I'm sad that Mamá still isn't with us, and that my grandma's still in Poland with my brothers and sister . . . and that only your brother will make it to the wedding from your side of the family too. This wretched war!'

Otto put his arms around her and kissed her. It was true – the war had ruined so much. But then again . . . if it hadn't been for the war he wouldn't have been in Elsen, and they wouldn't have met.

Erika seemed to be thinking the same. 'You know, Otto,' she told him, lost in her thoughts, 'if the German Reich still existed, we wouldn't be celebrating our engagement this Thursday. God doesn't make mistakes . . . even if we don't understand his ways sometimes.'

'You're right, my love. And we'd do well to remember it. Until death do us part . . . that's our promise to each other.'

'Until death do us part.'

The engagement was a happy occasion, even though there weren't many people there. The farm work was organised to allow for a longer evening. There was good food and – thanks to Aunt Toni – good wine too. And despite the general scarcity they received presents from the farmer and his wife, and from Erika's father, and from Otto's brother Emil – who'd got in touch with them recently – as well as a few local people.

But it was the postman who delivered the best surprise of all – a letter from Grandma Luise in Hörde saying that she and her three grandchildren had been released from the Polish camp and, after a brief stay in transit camp, had moved back into the apartment in Beukenberg Street. She was hoping to meet with other relatives soon. She also asked for news of her daughter Greta.

The mention of her mother brought fresh tears to Erika's eyes. But then she recalled Otto's words when they'd first met with her father: 'With God nothing is impossible.'

As they parted at the end of the day, Otto said, 'I'm sure she'll be here for the wedding.'

'That would be the second best gift of all,' she whispered.

'And the best?' Otto asked.

'Silly boy – you of course! Now goodnight, my sweet!' And with one last kiss she disappeared behind her door.

Otto stood in front of her door a moment longer – a door that would remain closed to him for seven more months. Could he wait? Yes, with God's help. It wasn't always easy to be sleeping next door and maintain self-control, not for either of them. But God was helping them in this too – of that he had no doubt.

In the spring of 1949 Otto began to look for a job and a place to live somewhere near Dortmund. He didn't want to stay on the farm for ever. After the wedding in May he wanted a steady job with reasonable hours, not one that began at five o'clock every morning and often went on till late at night. And a weekend too! Certainly they'd need Sundays so that they could get to church and meet other Christians.

It wasn't easy being the only Protestants in the Catholic Paderborn district. But surely God's promise that he would help them had to hold for this situation as well. Again and again they prayed, individually and as a couple, for a job, for a place to live, for a church. He would help them.

And so he did. Eventually Otto found a job at a metalworks factory that wasn't earmarked for demolition after the war. In fact it was due for expansion. What's more, the Russian workers who'd been forced to work there had long since been released, so there was even accommodation available. The barracks apartments were mostly still there, which gave Otto the chance to sign up for a relatively large room.

And so, on the 1st April 1949, Otto packed his bags, bid a tearful goodbye to Erika, who'd be joining him in a few weeks, and moved into their new place. Meanwhile Erika gave her notice to the farmer and his wife, sad to be leaving. Chances were they would never meet again. But who could say? The whole world was changing.

The last goodbye came on the 1st May, at Paderborn Station. Margret and Inge couldn't hold back the tears, even though they both understood that a woman had to be with her man. As Erika waved through the train window she knew another chapter in her life was over.

For the next few days, until her wedding day on the 7th May, Erika would be spending the time with her grandma and her brothers and sister in Hörde. If only her mother could be there too, her happiness would be complete.

It didn't take long to get from the station to Beukenberg Street. The thought of finally seeing Grandma, Hellmuth, Hildegard and Siegfried gave her wings. And so she walked the last hundred metres on air, right up to the ruins of her parents' home, where the ground floor had been rebuilt. It looked quite presentable. Her spirits lifted even higher as she approached. The trees and bushes seemed extra green somehow, the birds sounded extra sweet. She took in the bright yellow of the daffodils and the warm reds of the tulips. Had they always been there, or did it have something to do with the wedding?

Even from the street Erika could hear voices in the garden behind the house. Her loved ones were outside, enjoying the beautiful spring weather. She decided to creep behind the house and surprise them. She stood by the corner of the house and peeped round. What she saw made her jaw drop and her heart almost stop. There, sitting round the table, she saw her grandma, and the youngsters except Siegfried . . . and her mother.

With her bags flung aside and a cry of *Mamá! Mamá!* on her lips, she ran into the scene. The next moment mother and daughter were hugging each other, crying and laughing at the same time. Neither wanted to let go.

'And what about us?' It was her sister, Hildegard. 'I want a hug too!'

'Me too!' Hellmuth chimed in. Erika threw her arms around them, one by one, finishing with Grandma Luise.

They told their stories late into the night. Her mother had been deported to Siberia shortly after Erika left. She'd had to work underground in a mine, where many of her fellow workers had died of hunger, exhaustion, cold, or sickness. When Erika whispered a question to her mother about 'special services' for the men, she was evasive. 'I'm just happy to have escaped that hell, though it will be years before the memory goes away – if it ever does.'

Grandpa Kiel had been buried by the Polish and Grandma Luise and her grandchildren had been taken to a camp near Posen. Erika's little brother Siegfried had caught tuberculosis there and was still in a sanatorium where he was going to have to stay for some time yet.

When it grew too chilly to be outside they continued over dinner and on into the evening, until they were tired enough for bed. *Mamá*, who didn't seem to mind the French form of address any more, made room for Erika and happily shared her blanket.

Erika was overwhelmed by the events of the day. She had prayed for her mother to be back for the wedding, and now here she was! This was going to be some event! Erika wondered if Otto had already got word about her mother. But they would meet soon enough, that Thursday night in Hörde, as Otto was allowed to take the Friday off. And once her father was there as well it was going to be a real squeeze – but even more amazing. She couldn't wait.

The days went by more quickly than she expected, filled as they were with the everyday things that had to be done under a single roof with three generations living together – not to mention the wedding preparations. And all this served a secondary purpose – to avoid the need to discuss the current political situation, which Greta in particular was loath to do. For her, the disappointment of the last few years was just too painful. Better to talk of weddings and the future!

The wedding party on the 7th May 1949.
Behind the bridal couple 4th from right: Arthur.
On the right of the bridegroom: Greta.
Front row: Hellmuth (extreme left), Hildegard (3rd from left),
Siegfried (2nd from right).

What a celebration they had on the 7th May 1949. The family was complete, as even Siegfried had been allowed to come. Arthur brought the meat for the wedding feast – he'd been allowed to feed up a pig which had been duly slaughtered. Soup, potatoes, vegetables, meat, good wine . . . and afterwards chocolate pudding! For a few moments the war was forgotten.

Later they had cake and coffee – so much of it thanks to Aunt Toni, whose parcels had enabled them to buy things on the black market. If only she'd been able to come to the wedding, thought Erika. But Aunt Erna was there, and handed the young couple a beautifully decorated text of the twenty-third psalm.

Amazingly that turned out to be the very text the happy couple had chosen for the service and which the pastor had preached on. 'Always be guided by the Good Shepherd,' he had said, 'because he only leads us in good ways. And don't be fearful, even in the dark valleys. They're part of everyone's life. But God is always there to help, to comfort, and to bless.' Then he closed with this thought: 'Remember the ultimate goal: to dwell in the house of the Lord for ever!'

It was a wonderful message. The picture with the text of the psalm would hang on the wall of their apartment as a constant reminder that Someone held their lives in his hand. The Good Shepherd would be with them 'till death do us part'.

Otto and Erika as a young married couple
in front of their barracks accommodation in 1950.

Afterword

Now, after more than half a century, that vow still holds and Erika is still Otto's 'sweetheart'. Back in 1949 none of them could have guessed that they'd be given so much time together. They didn't have all the children they dreamed of, but they were blessed with a daughter, and a house of their own, and they got to work in their large garden until their strength ran out. And they travelled around the country in times of lasting peace – another dream come true.

They found their spiritual home in a church and in the Union of the Blue Cross. The couple lived out the truth which they held just as dearly when they grew old: it's worth paying attention to all the psalms (and not just the well-known ones), to the prophets, and to other godly people. It's worth following the Good Shepherd and trusting in God's promises. This is the path of true contentment, living by the gospel of our Saviour Jesus, and with the certainty that –

> The Lord is with me; I will not be afraid.
> What can man do to me?
> The Lord is with me; he is my helper.

*Erika – thankful and happy,
in the woods near her home in 1953.*